THE

FUNNEL
PRINCIPLE

*What Every Salesperson
Must Know About Selling*

MARK SELLERS

Library of Congress Cataloging in Publication Data

Sellers, Mark
    The Funnel Principle: What Every Salesperson Must Know
about Selling
    Includes index.
    ISBN 978-0-9801902-0-5
        1. Selling. 2. Sales Management. 3. Consumer Behavior.

Library of Congress Control Number: 2007941731

Copies of The Funnel Principle are available for purchase at
www.funnelprinciple.com or www.breakthrough-sales.com.

Volume Rates are available upon request.

Contact Breakthrough SalesPerformance LLC at
614.571.8267 or info@funnelprinciple.com

Charting your own path means cutting the brush yourself.

Your destiny will not take place in a vacuum; it will require the participation of others.

- Harvey Hook

To Dad, the best salesman I know.

CONTENTS

Acknowledgments

I have some very special people to thank.

First, I want to recognize my wife Bonnie. You've been subjected to far too many 4:30 am writers' alarms than anyone should have to endure. Thanks for your patience. Your belief in me is unbelievably and constantly appreciated.

I thank the good people at Miller Heiman Inc. for allowing me to partner with the company for the past eleven years and be part of a great brand for sales training. I especially thank Diane Sanchez, former president of Miller Heiman who gave me my start as a sales consultant in 1996. You gave me the best advice when, after I expressed my excited interest in representing the company you said "Go knock yourself out." This career becomes what you make it.

A huge thanks goes to all of my clients. The experiences with you have made much of this possible. I have learned and gained so much from each engagement. Your confidence in me as a trusted advisor to your sales teams is a responsibility I don't take lightly.

The Funnel Principle is made possible because of the groundbreaking methods of several legends in this trade that preceded the book, at least the ones I am directly and intimately familiar with. Steve Heiman and Bob Miller, Mike Bosworth, Neil Rackham, Jim Holden,

Dale Carnegie, Larry Wilson, and the original Professional Selling Skills from Learning International (now Achieve Global).

I thank the sales consultant professionals I've been fortunate to learn from the past several years. We've enjoyed many beers, many stories, many laughs, and many travels. Thanks to Brian Dietmeyer for being generous with your time and insight. Thanks Tom Martin for helping during the early days.

Several others have contributed in important ways. Mr. Bob Shook was kind enough to help me with the title and provide great insight into the craft of writing. You taught me that writing these kinds of books is about having a conversation with the reader. I'm honored to know you. Thanks to Dr. Kevin Elko, a motivational speaker for introducing me to Bob. Thank you Bill Beausay, an accomplished author and great friend for your generosity of time and spirit. Thanks to Ron Cooper. The conversations we had were helpful and I greatly appreciate your time. Thank you Edie Driskill, author and entrepreneur for your insight into the writing business. And finally, thanks to April Goyer. You're a fantastic listener, passionate about me, and a great life coach.

I want to recognize two clients. Stu Spangler of the Goodyear Tire & Rubber Co. and Marv Raglon of Whirlpool Corp. Stu - You're the model of being a student of the craft of selling. You've been unbelievably generous with your time and insight about funnel management. I am better because of your interest in me.

I have a special affinity for you Marv. You were one of the toughest sales I ever made. Your tireless persistence helped us create lasting change in sales behavior for the salesforce of one of the world's best brands. You leave many legacies. Your high standards made me better. And you ride a pretty good motorcycle. I will dearly miss you being a part of my work with the Whirlpool Corp.

Introduction

In twelve years as a sales consultant to many of the world's most respected companies and recognizable brands the most common and most pressing need expressed to me by sales people, their managers and their senior sales leaders is the need to find, qualify, and win new business day after day. They're referring to this task in total – that is, finding, qualifying and winning not just one sale, but rather doing this throughout the year enroute to the thing that salespeople are expected to do – achieve quota. Getting to a required number of sales (quota), from a larger number of qualified leads, from an even larger number of leads overall. I call this entire function *sales funnel management*. Could there be a more important function for any business? And yet, despite the importance of sales funnel management to the success of the business, the absence of structured processes for this function is conspicuously absent.

As a result, I have developed a solution to this. The net solution is an 8-Step Funnel Management Process for creating a world class sales funnel management competency for business to business enterprises. The process centers around a new funnel model I've designed called the BuyCycle Funnel™. This model turns upside down the traditional sales funnel and confronts the casual approach to funnel management associated with it – an approach that is costing companies millions of dollars of lost sales and lost productivity every year.

What started as a novel idea several years ago, the BuyCycle Funnel™ has been validated by thousands of sales people and the companies they work for. Some of these companies are big – multi billion dollar enterprises with hundreds of sales people. Others are small with $10M in revenue and a handful of salespeople; some of the companies sell through direct channels and others sell through indirect channels; some sell services and others sell products. I've been fortunate to have the best lab one could imagine for this model – real clients with real needs.

Honestly, I didn't set out to create a new model for the funnel nor an 8-Step Funnel Management Process. I created the BuyCycle Funnel™ and the 8-Step Process in response to clients who asked me to help them improve their sales performance. I wanted satisfied clients and a successful consulting practice. I'm proud to say that since I founded Breakthrough SalesPerformance™ in 1996 I have both.

The BuyCycle Funnel™ has transformed the way my clients sell and manage their salesforces. My clients have increased their sales using it. They have documented better productivity. Their salespeople have benefited, and so have their managers, their senior executives, and even non sales staff who participate with sales in selling. Sales managers use the BuyCycle Funnel™ to better develop their salespeople and hit their numbers. Senior executives use it to forecast and plan better. Their successes and experiences are documented throughout the book. You'll learn a great deal from them.

Why the Funnel?

One question I get asked often is this: *"Does the funnel really play such an important role in better selling?"* The short answer is emphatically yes! You'll read all about the funnel as being an untapped tool, sold short, taken for granted and misunderstood. Making the BuyCycle Funnel™ pay off for you might demand an entirely new perspective on your part.

For the past 12 years I've consulted with hundreds of clients who mainly sell in a business to business arena. They sell in many different types of industries, different products and services and different channels. In all of these experiences I've seen lots of different kinds of sales problems, and the client usually has an idea of what it is. The client might state it as a prospecting issue or a close rate issue. They might say their sales people aren't closing well enough. They might say they're discounting too early and too much. They might say their funnels don't have enough going on in them. They might say they aren't growing new revenue in strategic accounts. Or they aren't spending enough time selling. And in a way they're all right.

But as a consultant my job is to clarify, to simplify diagnosis, and eventually to recommend solutions that are effective and reasonable to pull off. This stuff might not be rocket science, but it's amazing how much can get in the way of the truth and fact. In all of this client work I recognized patterns of ineffective selling that lead back to funnel related issues. Some of these patterns are within my clients' own salesforces, and some patterns are seen among all of my clients and their salesforces.

Eventually I identified two root causes of ineffective selling. These two root causes surfaced the more I understood how my clients approached their two fundamental functions of the sales job, which are: 1) working a lead from start to finish, and 2) working enough leads for a certain percentage of them to close to hit the sales quota for the year. Because it's not always easy to know why your sales efforts are not working reducing to two root causes the real issues of ineffective selling helps clients simplify the complexity of their unique problems. Better solutions and better sales performance followed.

Eventually I started asking people about their funnel processes. Most of them would refer to their sales funnel (e.g. pipeline) or funnel process in explaining to me how they worked a lead. In working a lead, their funnel was their selling process and it had defined stages or milestones. The stages at the bottom of the funnel were close to being an order. Stages at the top of the funnel were new leads. Their *selling process*, defined collectively by all of the funnel stages, would tell them where each sales opportunity was toward becoming a sale, which then told them what selling activity they should do next.

When I asked how they knew if they were prospecting enough for new leads and if they had enough on their funnels to achieve their sales objectives the answers varied from *'not a clue'* (at least they were honest) to *'I've got enough'* to *'what do you mean?'* What they almost always couldn't do was tell me with high confidence *why they responded the way they did*. It didn't matter what the answer was – they didn't know how they arrived at it. This alone was a breakthrough for many clients – they were sharp enough to know that the first step to improving sales success was knowing what they did well, and how, and what they didn't do well, and why. Having a great year might be nice that year, but if you don't know how you produce your success today then how will *re-produce* it tomorrow?

This question about prospecting enough is related to funnel value, which is the dollar value of the sales opportunities on someone's funnel. Funnel value is something most salespeople intuitively know they need to know, but most don't have a reliable way to measure it. In other words, they need to know the answer to the question their managers often ask, *"Are you working enough deals?"* Some people counted the dollar value of all the deals on the funnel while others counted only some deals. If you are to maximize your chances of hitting quota year after year, and practicing good funnel management, it's important to know *what deals* to count and even more important to know how to count them. For example, if the funnel value is too small you'll have to add more deals to your funnel or bump up the dollar value of the deals you're currently working. If the funnel value is sufficient you'll need to know which part of your funnel and even which opportunities deserve your attention first.

In the funnels I saw and the conversations I had about the function I found that by far the most common approach to valuing the funnel used a design that was based on selling activity. It wasn't obvious at first that this was part of the problem. But there's an inherent problem with a selling activity-based funnel design - it is defined by what the *salesperson* does, not by what the *customer* does. Your sales efforts are focused on your selling process, not the customer's buying process. A selling process focus promotes ineffective behavior such as not learning enough or the right things about the customer's needs. It encourages you to commit to selling activities that shouldn't be done at all or done yet depending on where the customer is in the buying process. It tempts you to not get customer commitment, and yet committing lots of your own time, money and energy – and that of your staff's - in the sale. It often leads to an overstated funnel value – you think your funnel has enough activity on it to achieve your quota by year's end. In summary, a selling activity-based funnel design sets in place an ineffectiveness of funnel management that leads to longer sales cycles, lower sales productivity, lost sales, and missed forecasts. Sure makes for a rotten day.

The BuyCycle Funnel™ turns this selling activity-based approach upside down by *designing the funnel by the customer's buying process or buying cycle*. In the chapters that follow, you'll learn the details of the BuyCycle Funnel™, how it works, how to build one, and why it's the key to better funnel management and better selling. However – remember that as important as the BuyCycle Funnel™ is it's still just a funnel. Having the right funnel is just one part of the big picture of funnel management. To get to a world class competency you'll need a process. That's where the 8-Step Funnel Management Process comes in.

As with any new sales system, especially one that salespeople will be asked to adopt, it must be simple to understand and to implement. I learned this first as a salesperson selling for Johnson & Johnson and Pfizer and receiving high quality and usable training, then as a sales manager for a mid sized medical device firm, and now as a consultant working with clients. I took great pains to simplify how you use the BuyCycle Funnel™ and the 8-Step Process. I have to admit that at times I thought the simplicity implied weakness and lack of depth. I was reminded of the several excellent, beautifully simple selling methods that I have come to know intimately as a consultant and a student of the craft of selling. Strategic Selling from the Miller Heiman company was one. Solution Selling from the company of the same name was another one. Wilson Learning's Counselor Selling, and SPIN Selling from Huthwaite. These four methods have become standards of selling for millions of sales people largely on the strength of how simple and effective their methods are to understand and use. I was also driven by a quote attributed to Colin Powell that reads, *"Great leaders are able to simplify and provide solutions that anyone can understand."* I hope I've done that in The BuyCycle Funnel™ and the 8-Step Process.

Learnings, Outcomes and Payoff

By the time you finish this book you will have a new perspective on the role the funnel plays in your business. You'll learn that sales funnel management is a business function that deserves an investment in process, an investment that can pay off in higher revenues and productivity. You'll learn that the common, traditional funnel design today is not only flawed, but it can do more harm than good. You'll learn a new funnel model, the BuyCycle Funnel™, but you'll also learn that the real payoff requires much more than just a better funnel model, the 8-Step Process for Funnel Management. Adopting this approach will take commitment from many stakeholders to make that investment pay off in the form of a world class funnel competency. The outcomes are too important to be left to chance.

My goal is to educate, excite and equip you with the inspiration to act and the know how to execute. I'm confident that with your dedicated practice and commitment to adopting the approach you can transform your sales performance, that of your sales team's, or that of your entire organization. Let's begin in Part One with the basics – what is a funnel and what is it used for, and what is the most common approach to this tool and function today.

Good selling,

Mark Sellers

Part One:

A Sales Funnel Primer

Chapter 1

The Function of a Funnel

My name is Mark Sellers and I want to transform the way you sell.

I'm going to do this by helping you be more successful in the one mission that stands out for you, year after year in this career – achieving your quota. I'll help you master the function that has more impact on this mission than any other that you do – managing your sales funnel.

I've developed a new model for the funnel that's called the BuyCycle Funnel™ and it's part of an approach I've developed called the 8-Step Process for Funnel Management. The BuyCycle Funnel™ is a proven model for making significant improvement in sales funnel management and sales performance – you'll hear about clients that have validated it and that have transformed their selling approaches using this system.

For some of you, you'll be revisiting a familiar topic in the funnel since you may have a funnel already or have used one in the past. For others, the model and system will break new ground for you. For all of you, the BuyCycle Funnel™ and the 8-Step Process can give you the edge in your selling to take you to the next level.

Why the Funnel?

I know what some of you are thinking. Sales funnel… Been there… Got one of those. Thank you very much Mark, I'll be seeing you!

Hold on just a second. You may think you know all you need to know about the funnel. You might know a lot. You might use a funnel or a sales pipeline right now. You might even have parts of a funnel process. Business may be just fine for you - I truly hope it is. I'm not here to argue or show you how much I know. I'm here as a sales guy to share with you a way to be systematic and disciplined about what is arguably (now I am arguing) the most important responsibility you have as a salesperson – to find, qualify and win new business day after day, month after month, throughout the entire year in pursuit of achieving quota.

I realize that last statement is bold. It's just that I've seen exciting results for people and their companies after they've applied the BuyCycle Funnel™. These are people and companies that already had a lot of success in selling by the time I met them. To their credit, many of them rededicated themselves to understanding the funnel and, after initial skepticism, set aside long held perceptions of what a funnel is and what it does.

For some salespeople, applying the BuyCycle Funnel™ turned around an average year. For some sales managers, it transformed how they coach and develop salespeople. For heads of sales like the VP it's given them a visibility to the health or state of their business that they've never had before. Many of them have adopted a new way to forecast and are more accurate at it. I've sat in on CEO staff meetings and heard senior leaders comment on the integrity of the funnel data that the BuyCycle Funnel™ provides, which helps them better diagnose and make better business decisions. How one tool impacts so many different levels of responsibility and even different departments speaks to the untapped potential of the funnel, in general. The funnel connects the entire chain of sales – from the territory up through the VP or head of sales – and also connects other parts of the business such as marketing, new product development, sales support staff, senior management and the CFO.

While the funnel holds great potential as a tool for the entire business, the business relies on the fundamental need to have each salesperson achieving his or her own sales objectives, one territory at a time. How is the funnel such a valuable tool to achieving the territory sales goals? A VP of Sales of a client of mine told it to me this way: "The sales funnel is the most underused, misunderstood and misused tool with the greatest potential in business today," he said. "I tell my sales people that the sales funnel holds the answer to the question of the day – the one question they need to be asking themselves every day:

> **"What is your funnel's ability right now to close enough business to hit your quota this year?"**

He continued. "As long as they're working for me, this is why my sales people exist. If they ever lose sight of this question, shame on them – it won't be because of me. If the answer is, "I don't know," then we've got a problem. And we get to work. If the answer is, "Not as good as it needs to be," then we get to work. But we know what we're dealing with. If the answer is, 'It's looking good, boss," then I force them to tell me very clearly why they state that. The funnel doesn't lie. It tells a rep where he stands and what he needs to do. It takes the mystery - and the bullshit - out of what a rep must do to hit his number for the year."

In so many words, I couldn't agree more.

A New Perspective on the Funnel

One of the challenges I have is to convince you that funnel management is much more than simply having a funnel. The funnel, when designed correctly, is like a great race car that has the potential to blow every other car off the track. But the car doesn't drive itself. It needs a skilled and patient driver; it needs a top notch pit crew; and it needs a well-managed team. They all have to work well together to win the race. The funnel holds great potential, but it needs a process investment to realize its potential. If you're in sales, so many parts of your responsibility and the business overall are affected by how well you manage the funnel, including top-line sales, sales productivity, and forecasting. Many constituents are depending on you to succeed in each of these areas, and it's much more possible to succeed in them with the right funnel process. If you supply the commitment, we'll supply the process.

I've also got to convince you that the so-called traditional funnel design is actually part of the root cause of funnel problems. I'll show you that it makes no sense to design a funnel this traditional way, and therefore, makes no sense to build a funnel management process around a deficient funnel design. This might be risky on my part to suggest this, but I think that clear heads will prevail. Our better funnel design, the BuyCycle Funnel™, combines the concept of a buying process with the concept of the funnel. We didn't invent the funnel, and we didn't introduce the concept of a buying process. I'll reference later the people who deserve the credit for that. But I am the first to combine the two concepts into a simple-to-use, easy-to-understand approach - our 8-Step Funnel Process.

Proven Effective

I'm confident that a BuyCycle Funnel™ design and the 8-Step Process can have a significant impact on your business for several reasons.

One, clients have proven it. Over several years, they've validated the effectiveness of using the BuyCycle Funnel™ – highly recognized companies such as Whirlpool, Honeywell, Goodyear, and Smith & Nephew, and many other companies in various industries and of various sizes. These clients and others routinely experienced documented increases in sales and sales productivity, strategic account penetration, and more salespeople achieving quota.

Two, the BuyCycle Funnel™ is easy to understand and implement.
I've learned that getting salespeople to adopt new ways of selling
is tough. If the way isn't easy to understand and implement it
won't be used. In designing the BuyCycle Funnel™ and the 8-Step
Process, I looked to well-respected, highly regarded sales methods
for inspiration to making it simple. Miller Heiman's Strategic Selling
course was one. Solution Selling was another one. SPIN Selling
by Huthwaite was a third one. And Counselor Selling by Wilson
Learning was a fourth. These four methods broke new ground in
selling effectiveness largely because they were (and still are) simple
to use. Many of my BuyCycle Funnel™ clients have used me to
incorporate SPIN Selling or Solution Selling or Strategic Selling or
other sales methods into their funnels. The funnel becomes the
overriding process while the selling method is the lever to accelerate
and reliably execute the BuyCycle Funnel™. I talk more about this in
a later chapter.

Three, it builds on a base that most salespeople are familiar with.
I'm not inventing the sales funnel - I'm just offering a better design to
the traditional funnel and most importantly putting a simple process
to using it. If you're familiar with the funnel concept, then adopting
the 8-Step Process will be a logical next step for you and a path to
greater productivity and performance.

Four, I practice what I preach. I heard my mother say once, be
wary of the cook who doesn't eat her own food. For twelve years,
I've steadily grown a successful sales consulting practice of mostly
Fortune 500 clients and I attribute that to working my own BuyCycle
Funnel™. While I am not modest about my sales talents (everyone's
talented at something), I am humbled by the accomplishments.

I said earlier that achieving a world class funnel competency with the
8-Step Process and BuyCycle Funnel™ will require a new perspective
of the funnel as a tool to build a specific kind of process around,
and not just a tool that stands on its own. Like many of my clients,
you're probably familiar with the funnel to some degree. You might
have a funnel or pipeline or parts of a funnel process. You might

be reading this because you are intrigued rather than because your business is suffering. You might be looking for a new selling idea because you are a student of the craft. I commend you. When you acknowledge that changing the way you do something can be very hard, and that without continually changing, your performance over time can slowly suffer, you realize that staying on top of your sales game is no small feat. As my clients implemented the 8-Step Process and the BuyCycle Funnel™ some would say, *"I kind of do that already, but this puts it into a process that helps me understand it much better."* Bingo. The process gives you consistency. It exposes the true cause and effect of your selling efforts. Let's face it – if you don't know why you are successful then how will you replicate your success in the future?

Here are some questions to ask yourself as you take this journey:

- *What is my process for finding, qualifying and winning new sales opportunities day in and day out?*

- *How effective am I in using the process?*

- *How is my effectiveness with it measured?*

- *What do I do with that information to improve?*

- *What part of the process can I focus on to have immediate lift to my sales performance?*

There's a big difference between *knowing* something and *doing* something. And, a big difference between doing something well and doing it well consistently. Many of the sales challenges you face might be due to breakdowns in simple execution of fundamental sales behaviors, rather than due to not knowing what you should be doing. Our 8-Step Process and the BuyCycle Funnel™ will give you the know-how and the path to consistent execution of an effective funnel process to achieve your sales goals.

Although the BuyCycle Funnel™ is an effective and innovative model, the key to being successful with it is committing to the 8-Step Process on a daily basis. You'll learn how to do that in the book. I tell you everything you need to know to get started, to implement it, to sustain it, and to measure its effectiveness. For example, you'll need to be disciplined in keeping track of your funnel activity. You or your sales manager need to regularly inspect the funnel. You'll have to set goals to make sure you're giving the right attention to the right parts of your funnel. And, if you're a VP of Sales, you can create a process where all territory funnels roll-up to you and give you a visibility and quality of funnel data to make better predictions about future revenue and make better business decisions.

In this opening chapter you'll learn the following:

1. What a funnel is and what it can do for you.

2. The common sales related problems facing sales people and why the right funnel process is the best way to address these common problems.

3. What a traditional funnel looks like and why it's flawed.

4. How the BuyCycle Funnel™ is a meaningfully different model from a traditional funnel and why that's important to your sales success.

What Is a Funnel?

Let's start with the fundamentals. A funnel is simply your list of active sales opportunities. As a salesperson, your world revolves around putting new sales opportunities in the top of the funnel, working them through the process, and winning your fair share. Since you don't win everything that enters your funnel you have to constantly find new leads. Some sales people know

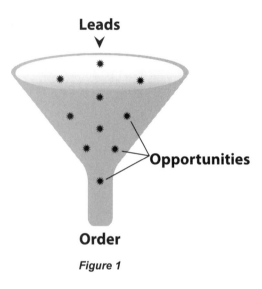

Leads

Opportunities

Order

Figure 1

exactly how many opportunities they need to be actively pursuing for one lead to end up as an order. That's a good start. And, it's just one best practice that I'll put process to that will help you be more consistent and effective.

You can think of your funnel as being tangible and in a physical place. Usually funnels are kept in excel spreadsheets or in software programs that also serve as contact management tools. The spreadsheets or software lets you not only see your funnel, section by section, but also run reports. Keep in mind that the reports and the software help you use your funnel process. They're not the funnel process itself.

Also, your account list is not your funnel. Your funnel is a funnel of opportunities, not accounts. You might have more than one or even several opportunities within one account.

What You Can Funnel

If you're a salesperson, it's easy to see that you have a funnel. But there are many other parts of the business that can also be funneled.

What You Can Funnel

Sales Territory Funnel

Midwest
Territory

Region Sales Funnel

Western
Region

National Accounts Funnel

All
Contracts

Strategic Accounts Funnel

$15B Medical
Supplies
Company

Product Funnel for Marketing

$5M Widget
Sales

Figure 2

A Sales Region or District

If you're a sales manager of salespeople, you can have a funnel for your region. It's comprised of all of the funnels of the salespeople you manage. If you're a director of sales and you manage sales managers who manage sales people, you can have a funnel comprised of the funnels of your sales managers.

An Entire Salesforce

If you're a VP of sales, your funnel can be for the entire salesforce. All of the sales territory funnels roll up to you. You have visibility of all of the sales opportunities being pursued, and you can run reports on that business to help you diagnose and forecast and make good business decisions. The heads of sales of most of my clients cite this visibility as something they've never had before and are thrilled to now have it.

A National Accounts Funnel

If your company sells in a market where you contract with large organizations that represent, to some degree, a constituent base of companies or locations or branches that you then sell to, you will want to manage that business with a sales funnel. These accounts are sometimes called national accounts. This is a common way to sell for many types of companies. For example, a healthcare company that sells to hospitals has to get contracts with buying groups called GPOs (group purchasing organizations), where a GPO might represent hundreds of hospitals. Another example is asset management firms that sell their products, stock or bond funds, to brokers and dealers, insurance companies or banks. They try to get their funds 'in the model' or on a platform that the customer, the end-user that buys a fund from the insurance company or wirehouse, then selects. Once you're in the model, the firm's salesforce in the field, referred to as wholesalers calls on these broker/dealers and banks and other companies to promote the fund that is now available to that company's advisors. And providing one more example, if you're in the building trade selling to home builders you might have a national accounts group that sells to these companies such as DR Horton, Toll Brothers or Centex Homes. Having contracts with these national builders is a necessary step in selling to their local branches and winning the projects they are working on.

Having a funnel for national accounts activity helps in several ways. One, the seller is trying to land contracts throughout the year. A funnel drives this activity. Two, the seller can be more effective with a joint or aligned effort of its national accounts and territory field salespeople and use the funnel to drive this alignment. The company can also direct its territory-based salespeople toward the accounts that fall under one of their major contracts for revenue or strategic or other sales goals. Three, the manufacturer can track the selling efforts in certain accounts and report that activity to the customer to demonstrate activity level and commitment. I devote an entire chapter to using a funnel system for these types of accounts.

A Strategic Accounts Funnel

Some companies have accounts that represent a large percentage of their overall sales, sort of the 80/20 situation or some version of that. Because these accounts bring in lots of business and/or profits they deserve special attention. They get increased investments of time and resources. And, at the end of the day, the goal is often to sell more to these accounts. Having a funnel process to do this is one of the best investments a company can make.

One of my early clients was a multibillion dollar industrial products company with eight large divisions. It was common to see more than one division selling to one large customer such as John Deere or Applied Industrial Technologies. While some divisions were doing well selling to the large customers, others were not. There was no coordinated selling effort among the divisions. Senior management had an interest in knowing activities and sales in-progress in these accounts, but it had no visibility to this. They knew this was not an effective way to protect and grow the overall business in these accounts. They implemented a strategic account process by appointing managers dedicated to the accounts and then hired me to create and implement a funnel process to manage the sales activity. The result was an increase in sales and a visibility to that part of its business that they'd never had.

A Product Line Funnel

While it's easy to see that you can funnel something related to the sales organization, you can also apply funnel management to marketing. Product managers obviously want to increase sales and grow their brands. Managing their business using a funnel helps them do this. They can track sales opportunities in progress. A funnel helps them forecast sales for their products. It helps them allocate time to strategic sales opportunities that require special resources and extra effort. The funnel helps a product manager not only get more involved in selling; it helps him or her get involved in the right way. This adds value to the selling efforts.

A sales funnel simply helps you put focus on the selling efforts for a specific area or part of your business. Let's define exactly how a funnel helps you do this.

Function of a Funnel

A funnel has two functions:

1. It helps you work a sales lead from discovery to close, or until it's lost, or it's no longer viable.

2. It helps you accurately know what your funnel's ability is at any time to close enough new business to achieve your quota for the year, and to set a plan for doing so.

Let's look closer at each of these two functions.

Function 1: Work a Sales Lead from Discovery to Close

When you work a lead, you work it through the selling process until you close it, or you lose it, or the customer changes its mind about buying anything. The funnel helps you define *where* that opportunity is in that process. Knowing where it is helps you know what you need to do next. How? All funnels have stages or sections. A lead progresses through these stages to ultimately come out

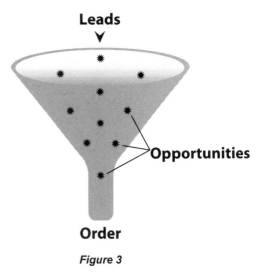

Leads

Opportunities

Order

Figure 3

the bottom as an order. For example, a very common first stage of the funnel is something like 'make an introduction' or 'send product literature.' After you do that with a prospect, your funnel stages tell you what you should next. If in your business you have product samples or you do demonstrations of software you might have a stage called 'provide a sample' or 'do product demonstration.' And, another stage further down the funnel might be called 'submit a proposal.' You'd do that when you thought that a prospect was serious enough about making a purchase. *In theory*. We'll see later, it doesn't always work this way.

Function 2: Manage All Opportunities

The second function plays another important role in your sales responsibility. It tells you at any time during your year what your funnel's ability is to close the business you need to close to hit your numbers. For example, if you have a $1M quota and you've closed $600,000 by June, and you're on a fiscal calendar year, you need to know the answer to a simple question, *"Do you have enough on your funnel to close another $400,000 by December 31 and hit your quota?"*

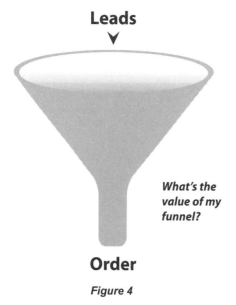

Leads

What's the value of my funnel?

Order

Figure 4

This leads to another important question you need the answer to and it may not be that obvious: how are you getting the answer to the question, *"What is your funnel's ability to achieve quota?"* I've seen some interesting approaches to this. Many of them rely on a gut feel with little or no defined or systematic approach. Each salesperson is allowed to come up with his or her system and forecast as he or she sees fit. Another approach is to put a dollar value on the funnel opportunities, but by using a funnel that's designed by selling activity. The outcomes are often inconsistent and infected with incorrect data.

Common Selling Mistakes that a Funnel Addresses

Without a funnel process, salespeople are prone to committing some common selling mistakes such as the following:

They wait too long to ask the question, "What's my funnel's ability right now to close enough business to hit my quota?" By the time they ask it, it's often too late – the funnel doesn't have enough activity to close that additional business and they're too late in the year to find enough new opportunities to make up the gap.

They fail to prospect enough because they're looking at a funnel full of bad funnel data. For the funnel to tell you if you're working enough deals to hit quota for the year, it has to have good funnel data. Meaning, the opportunities you're looking at must be *placed* at the right stage of the funnel. The problem is some opportunities *appear* to be further along the sales process than they really are because salespeople aren't looking at them the right way, from the customer's perspective. The funnel can look like it has enough activity in it. The reality is it has bad data and the problem isn't discovered until it's too late to do anything about it. The salesperson hasn't prospected enough throughout the year, and now no amount of prospecting will help him recover fully.

It seems that this is a simple issue to deal with. As long as you keep prospecting, you should have nothing to worry about, right? That might be fine if prospecting was the only task you had. The problem is you have other funnel tasks - tasks that your prospecting results in such as qualified leads. Some of these leads advance and you end up doing finals presentations and delivering lengthy proposals and big presentations and more. So the question on the minds of every salesperson is, how much prospecting should I do? Most sales people I've worked with, and their sales managers, don't really know. Sales data alone won't tell you, though that's the place many people go to find the answer. So you're 47% to plan and it's May. That's a lagging indicator. It's past and there's nothing you can do about it. With no process that diagnoses the funnel's ability to bring in future revenue managers resort to a strategy of screaming - Prospect! Prospect! Prospect! Unfortunately, the screaming loses effectiveness when the salesperson is out of earshot. Our system fixes this.

They hang on to deals that are dead. Dead at least for now. For some of these deals they are literally wishing and hoping them to be real. Wishing is wasted effort and leads to lower sales productivity. They should replace these deals immediately with new ones where the prospect commits to meaningful dialogue, truly has pain, funding to fix it and the energy to see the sale through.

They expect too much new business to come from existing customers and existing relationships. I'm all for retaining customers and if possible selling them more product and services if they have a need. I'm also for constantly finding new customers. Without new customers, it's only a matter of time before these existing relationships simply dry up with add-on or upselling opportunities.

All leads get equal attention. Bad move here because some leads are much more attractive than others. The attractive ones you're likely to win more easily and even faster. You're likely to have fewer post sale problems. If you eliminate the below average leads from your attention and invest your selling time in attractive leads, you'll improve your hit rate and sales productivity.

But this discernment is a tough task. For one, qualifying a lead is sometimes like a treasure hunt where you don't have all of the clues. You make decisions to pursue or not based on what you know, and often you're information deprived. It's easy to go down a wild goose chase. You might make assumptions about the authority or influence of the people you meet. And, just because a contact acknowledges a problem doesn't mean he's committed to doing something about it. Doing something about a problem takes energy. It's often easier to live with what they know – even when they know it's not right. Also, if your contact gets emotional about the issue, it's easy for you to get emotional too. You forget to stay rational about the opportunity and begin making all kinds of assumptions. When you're in the heat of the hunt these kinds of mistakes are easy to make.

You spend too much time on leads that are well-developed. This may sound counterintuitive. But I've seen too many sales people convince themselves that these deals need constant attention. If the salesperson has only one or two deals at this stage there's more pressure to win them. However, the reality is these deals often don't need as much selling time as you think. Or better said, you can easily keep busy tending to the needs of these deals and not have much of an incremental effect on winning them. And, when you spend too much time here, what takes a back seat? That's right – finding new leads and qualifying the good ones.

The good news is the BuyCycle Funnel™ and the 8-Step Process will help you address these problems.

We've defined a funnel, described its two functions and listed common sales problems that a funnel can address. Because the funnel is a tool that salespeople have used for some time, there's one design that has evolved as the generally accepted model. However, despite its widespread acceptance this *traditional model* not only doesn't help you perform your funnel functions as well as you need, it also can cause you more harm than good. In the next chapter you'll learn how the traditional funnel is flawed and why that works against you. Then, you'll discover a different model that should become the standard for your funnel management process going forward - the BuyCycle Funnel™.

Chapter 2

The Traditional Funnel

My dad is an expert – someone with great knowledge and skill in a particular thing. He has a lot of expertise, but one in particular is fixing things. He can fix cars because he used to take them apart and put them back together when he was younger. He can fix things around the house. He's built a few and he knows a lot about them. He's still fixing and working on things today. He recently rebuilt my brother's 1971 BMW motorcycle. As you might expect, I keep him pretty busy around my house when he visits me and my family.

You're in sales and you know something I'm going to state - you need to be an expert at it. I tell clients in my seminars *"you have to be a student of your craft."* Your success depends on it. Your customers deserve it. How do you do that? *Take the time to understand how selling works.* Now, there are many different *competency areas* of this great career such as making effective sales calls, strategically working the set of decision makers for a sale, effective presentations, time and territory management, negotiating, strategic account management, and, yes, funnel management. One way to start to be the student of your craft is to read everything you can get your hands on about selling. Learn to distinguish between the good fundamental concepts and ones that don't add much to your skill set. Challenge daily how to sell. Every sales call. Every sale. Evaluate every so-called good relationship. Is it the relationship or what you contribute to the relationship that's the reason people buy from you? This kind of scrutiny will make you a better salesperson and will take you wherever you want to go.

With the BuyCycle Funnel™ and the 8-Step Process you can become an expert at sales funnel management. You'll use the 8-Step Process to get there and the BuyCycle Funnel™ is the foundation of that process. Both components will help you learn, diagnose and set action plans. You'll get smarter about what's working and why.

To help you become a funnel expert, I'm going to take you on a walk through what I call the traditional way of managing a funnel. The more you know about this traditional approach the better you'll understand the BuyCycle Funnel™ and how to get the most from it. I'll tell you right now though that this traditional approach is not ideal. It's got some serious flaws. It makes it harder for you to be successful. But it's been around forever. Every one of my clients that had a funnel used a traditional design. Despite the traditional funnel's prevalence, I'm confident you'll come to the same conclusion I did about the ineffectiveness of this design.

Defining the Traditional Funnel

The defining characteristic of a traditional funnel is the stages are defined by *selling activities*. Examples include but are not limited to the following:

- Send literature
- Conduct an email campaign
- Provide samples
- Conduct a site visit
- Do a demonstration
- Do a trial or evaluation
- Do a needs assessment or analysis
- Make a sales call
- Make a major presentation

- Do a mock up
- Prepare a business case
- Send a proposal or quote
- Respond to an RFP or RFQ or RFI
- Do a finals presentation
- Negotiate terms and conditions

As you work a lead from discovery of the lead to a sale, you move that lead through stages like the ones above, one stage at a time. For example, one of the first things you might do to discover a new lead is **send literature** or **do an email campaign** to target prospects. You might target existing customers to sell them a new product or service that complements other products and services they currently buy from you. Depending on the response from one of these prospects, your next step might be to **make a sales call**. That call may lead to calls with other people at the account to learn their needs too. If they stay interested enough, in your opinion, your next step might be to **do a demo** or **provide a trial** or **offer some samples** for use. Those

selling activities may lead to further sales calls with other people. You may need their buy-in or input for **preparing a business case or proposal**.

Your next step might be preparing a proposal. The prospect might even ask you to do this. Once they review it, with you or without you present, you might follow up to learn if they're ready to buy. They might want to send you over to purchasing or some other department

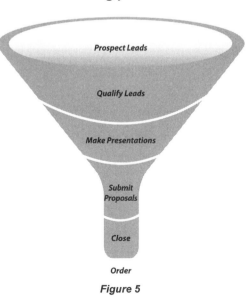

Traditional Funnel -
a selling process

Prospect Leads

Qualify Leads

Make Presentations

Submit Proposals

Close

Order

Figure 5

to **negotiate pricing, terms and conditions**. Next thing you know, you've made a sale. Life's good.

A Step in the Right Direction?

It's easy to think that defining a process for your selling like the one above could be a good thing. It gives you direction and focus. It helps you know the smaller goals you're trying to get to on the way to the big goal of making the sale. Given the typical long sales cycles and multiple people involved in a purchase decision for many business-to-business sales, it's hard to argue against a process that tries to put structure to that sales cycle. Sales people have come to know this as the 'selling process.'

> There's an inherent problem with defining a funnel using selling activity - you're focused on selling activity, not on the customer's buying process.

But what looks harmless is a wolf in sheep's clothing. There's an inherent problem with defining a funnel using selling activity - you're focused on *selling activity*, not on the *customer's buying process*. Whether or not you realize it, with a selling activity focus you get caught up in what you think you should do next in your selling efforts and can forget to think about what should the customer do next.

For example, in a traditional funnel it's common to have a stage called 'submit proposal.' At this stage you are supposed to prepare and submit a proposal to the customer. You've completed some other previous step in your selling process to get here. This is a significant step in the process for many reasons. The main one is because you believe the customer is ready to act on your proposal. A sale could be just around the corner. But wouldn't you want to know that the customer is genuinely ready to act on your proposal before spending hours or days preparing it? Sometimes the customer never intends to give you that shot at the business, even though they ask you for a proposal. They have other intentions. Maybe to use you to get the incumbent supplier to lower its price. Maybe to know for budget purposes what something like your product or service would cost. If you use 'submit proposal' as your funnel stage you could be misleading yourself on where the sale actually is in progress.

Remember that a proposal is a formal answer (yours) to a defined set of needs (the customer's) that the customer will decide to accept or not. It really is a big deal for both you and the customer. You have every right to ask questions to confirm the customer's intentions to act on it, including its timeframe and its process for reviewing it. If you don't probe and even challenge the customer to prove to you that it's ready to act on the proposal, be prepared to waste a percentage of your time on proposals that will never be acted on. Your sales productivity will take a hit.

One client of mine, a large healthcare products and services supplier, experienced this firsthand. The senior vice president told me about a large proposal his company submitted. They followed their sales process of responding to the RFP (request for proposal) once it was received. They had many internal meetings to discuss the opportunity and how to respond. They were well-organized. The problem was they were so eager to bid on this business that they refused to see the signs of a lack of real customer commitment to genuinely give them a shot at the business. They did ask about needs and decision-makers involved but didn't receive as much input as they would have liked. They went ahead and bid the business and submitted a proposal and invested several days preparing it. They sent it without requiring the customer to sit down and review it with them. Several months after sending the proposal, the customer still had not responded to anyone at my client. Why did they submit the proposal? He said it was the next step in their sales process after receiving the RFP.

So, what could they have done differently? The executive told me that if they were to do it again they'd consider not bidding the business unless the customer met some reasonable requests - *throughout the selling process.* For example, once they received the RFP they would have *required* more information. It's common that RFPs don't tell the whole story of customer needs. In most RFPs the seller is allowed to talk to people and get a better understanding of customer needs, even if the talks are limited to a vendor point person. Second, he said they would have requested meetings with the customer's senior executives. This was a large sale that had wide and deep implications for the customer. It's reasonable to think that senior executives on the customer side might be willing to share their vision and thoughts. If you were one of these customer senior executives and were counting on the reliability of a key supplier for hundreds of millions of dollars of business, wouldn't you take time to make sure your bidding suppliers understood the situation?

Another thing they'd have done different is strongly suggested a proposal review meeting. If a customer isn't willing to give you time to let you lead them through a review of your proposal, regardless of how big or small it is that's not a good sign of their intent to buy or feelings about your proposal.

I realize that just because you ask for these kinds of things along the sale you don't always get your requests granted. But, I also know that you're not likely to get something when you don't ask for it. By asking you improve your shot at getting what you need. There's another important benefit of selling this way. You condition the customer to expect that you'll expect them to share, engage and commit as a condition of the sale, throughout the process. Of course, they might laugh you out of the room. But let me ask you – how often do you win sales at your desired price and your desired margin with customers who don't play this way? How many sales to these types of customers have you won that you wished you hadn't made?

A sale doesn't have to be huge to see that a traditional funnel with stages defined by selling activity can have a dramatic impact on your effectiveness. For example, many of my clients have products that are sampled as part of the sale. During the course of the sale, usually early on, it's common for the customer to request a sample. This seems harmless until you find out how the samples are being used. The salesperson leaves a sample and then promises to return at some future time to see how the sample worked. In a perfect world, it would go like this:

Salesperson follows up on lead and meets customer

▼

Salesperson learns customer needs

▼

Customer wants to try the product

▼

Salesperson agrees and leaves a sample

▼

Customer tries product and product meets customer's expectations

▼

Customer places order for product

Maybe you know what often happens after the salesperson leaves a sample. He or she returns days or weeks later and sees the sample still sitting on the customer's desk, unused. The salesperson inquires about the use of the sample and the customer says he intends to get to it soon, he's been busy, he hasn't had time but he's surely still intending to try it, etc. The salesperson returns again a few days or weeks later and the sample is still there on the desk. Shame on those customers, right? If they say they'll use a sample then they should.

But, a good part of the blame goes to the salesperson who agrees to play this way – and yes, blame goes to a traditional funnel design that promotes a selling activity focus. The stage is likely called 'deliver sample.' Your job as the salesperson is to do just that. It's not a stretch to think that salespeople would believe that delivering samples results in sales, so the real selling never takes place. In other businesses, such as software sales, you can substitute sample for 'do demo.' Or, in some businesses the equivalent is 'get the evaluation.' Unfortunately, these well-intended selling resources are often misused by salespeople. They become crutches and obstacles to good selling.

Possibly, an even worse scenario, if you can believe that, is when the customer actually uses the sample. *What?* Isn't that the goal of leaving a sample? It is, and that's the problem. Simply leaving a sample puts all of the selling into that little box. What if they use it and tell you it just didn't work out? They say it didn't meet expectations. Well, what were the expectations? What was the real problem that the customer was hoping the sample experience to solve? What if you didn't take the time to ask that or even help the customer define those expectations before hand? This happens all the time. When you don't set these parameters in place for how something will be sampled or trialed, you set yourself up for failure.

A different approach to sampling is this: *Leave the sample in the car.* Talk to the customer and learn needs. Discover the consequences of those needs not being met, including dollars and cents, patient care, and the credibility of the people in the account letting problems persist instead of addressing them. Get the customer to commit to a very clear way and timing of using the sample. If he balks, maybe you haven't explained well enough the benefit of approaching the sample use this way – or maybe the customer isn't really committed to using it and eventually purchasing your product. If you are successful in revealing customer needs and then showing the customer how your products and solutions will address them, you don't want a sample to get in the way of that effectiveness. Get this – sometimes you'll even make a sale without using the sample.

There's nothing wrong with sampling per se. What's wrong is how the samples are sometimes used. When they're used in place of good fundamental selling, you won't be as effective. Your sales cycles will be longer. You won't make some sales.

An Ineffective Guide for What to do Next

There's a simple way to describe why a traditional funnel takes you off course. A funnel defined by selling activity is not the best guide for what you should do next in your selling efforts because it's not the best indicator of where the opportunity is on your funnel. In short:

> **You can't use selling activity to define the customer's buying process.**

Knowing where the customer is in the buying process is the key to more effective, more productive selling and funnel managing. Focusing on the buying process helps you know much better how the customer is going about the decision, including:

- Who's involved and what roles they play

- Who has the greatest influence

- Who has authority

- What the timing is for the decision

- What the personal motivations are for the people involved

- Where the funding is coming from and how much is available

- What the criteria is for selecting a new solution

- What problems exist

- Which problems are causing the most pain

- How long the problems have persisted and what's been done to correct them

Funnel Valuation Using a Traditional Funnel

How is a traditional funnel designed to help you with the second function, that is, managing all of your sales opportunities? And, why is it not the best approach?

First, let's be clear what we mean by managing all of the opportunities. As a salesperson, you have a quota to achieve. Throughout the year you compare what you've sold toward that quota to what you have left to sell to hit the quota. To know where you stand toward hitting quota you look at your funnel and ask,

> **"What is my funnel's ability right now to close enough business to hit my quota for the year?"**

Come Monday morning, with a million different things that will compete for your time and attention, you have to correctly choose which deals get your attention and how much time you devote to those deals. Do you spend time finding new leads? How much time? Do you revisit some deals that were hot for a while and then went cold? Sounds like time management. In a way it is, but I've come to believe that 'time' isn't what you're really managing. It's more about managing your sales priorities.

Since how you spend your time is so important, and that is determined by your funnel's ability right now to hit quota, what's the key to this sequence? *Your funnel needs to have good data.* Good funnel data means the opportunities are correctly *described* and *placed* at the correct funnel stage. For example, a deal that is worth $175,000 at stage 3 had better be listed on your funnel as a $175,000 deal at stage 3. However, what if it really belongs at stage two or stage one? If you have a funnel full of misplaced stage 3 opportunities that really belong in stage 2 or stage 1, you'll likely spend your time doing the wrong selling activities and will pay for this ineffectiveness down the road.

One client of mine found this out the hard way. A region manager with ten salespeople had a quota for a new product of less than $2M. Early in the year he believed that his region funnel for this one product had a value of $36 million. As you might expect he felt confident in his chances of hitting the quota. How much prospecting for new business do you think his salespeople should have been doing? Not much. With a funnel like this you should spend your time working the qualified deals and closing your fair share. With any reasonable close rate you'd expect his people to blast right through that quota. However, his $36 million funnel was significantly overvalued. The blame goes to a five-step traditional funnel the manager used. After we designed his BuyCycle Funnel™, we saw its true value fall to $5.6M. As you might expect, he was quite surprised, but to his credit, he understood where we were coming from. Unfortunately, his region ran out of time to get its funnel into better shape and at year's end the region missed its quota. Had they known earlier in the year the funnel value of $5.6 million, I know this manager would have required his people to spend a lot more time prospecting and working deals that were better qualified.

So, how did the traditional funnel give him a $36 million dollar false value? The manager did what is common to do. He added the dollar value of all of the opportunities on his funnel regardless of stage. We'll see in a second that this is one of three ways a traditional funnel is valued and is not the best approach.

Valuing the Funnel

How the funnel is valued is the key to the question *"What is my funnel's ability right now to close enough business to hit my quota for the year?"* Without any process, sales people might go to their funnels and ask themselves,

"What have I got going on?"

"What deals am I working?"

"What deals can I win?"

"Which deals do I have to win to hit quota?"

Or, they might value their funnels in one of the following ways:

Everything on the funnel is counted as funnel revenue. This is what our manager of the $36 million funnel did. Regardless of where the opportunity is, e.g. regardless of stage, the dollar value of each opportunity gets counted in the funnel value. For example, a sale worth $275,000 at any stage is counted as $275,000 toward the overall funnel value. Ten of those deals means you've got a $2,750,000 funnel. What's the problem with this? The deals that have just barely entered your funnel get the same value treatment as deals that have progressed well down the funnel. Even more specifically, deals where you've had one or two meetings in a long sales cycle get the same funnel valuation as deals where you've had several meetings, done your demos, confirmed funding and made group presentations. If that doesn't seem right, you're right. Your funnel will be overvalued.

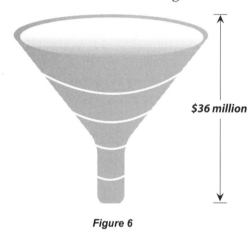

$36 million

Figure 6

Only sales that reach a certain funnel stage are counted toward the overall funnel value. For example, an opportunity that just made it to the funnel's first stage may not be counted in the funnel's dollar value. But one that gets far enough in the sales process does. For example, let's say you count toward funnel value those deals that reach stage 3 of your funnel. Let's say the funnel above has four of those $275,000 deals that have made it to the third stage and six deals that have not. That funnel's worth $1,100,000. While this is a step in the right direction it still is misguided. The flaw is in how the funnel stages are defined – as long as they are defined by selling activity the funnel is prone to giving bad data. The opportunities listed at the lower stages may not deserve to be there. Why are they there? Because of some selling activity you have done, not due to something the customer's done.

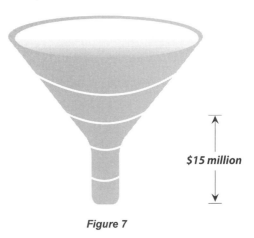

$15 million

Figure 7

The dollar value of each opportunity is based on a percentage that is applied to each opportunity at each stage. This is called a weighted funnel. For example, an opportunity at stage 1 might be given a 10% factor. An opportunity at stage 3 might be given 50%.

So, the $100,000 sale at stage 3 is valued at $50,000 for funnel purposes. This is probably the best of the three approaches, but it still has some shortcomings. Putting a partial dollar value on an opportunity suggests that you can win part of it. In sales you either win all of it or you lose it. Another problem is putting a partial dollar value on an opportunity that is at the very top of your funnel. This

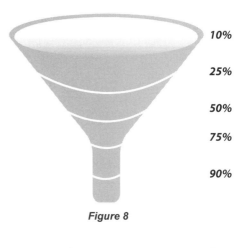

10%

25%

50%

75%

90%

Figure 8

implies that you know, with confidence, the dollar value of that opportunity. For my clients, deals that are early in discovery and that have just entered the funnel are too early to know the dollar value. Putting a dollar value on those deals is creating bad data and leads to an overvalued funnel.

The other danger in assigning a percentage likelihood of winning to each funnel stage is you are labeling all opportunities at each stage with the same percentage likelihood of closing. You are basing that on the one criterion that puts the opportunity at that stage. In reality, it's more likely that each opportunity has a different likelihood of being a sale because each one measures differently against criteria used to assess the likelihood. In other words, to get the real likelihood of an opportunity becoming an order, you'd need to run each opportunity through that stage criterion. For salespeople that have many opportunities on their funnels, it's not realistic to think they could do that kind of analysis on every one, and I'm not recommending it for that reason. But, for others that have fewer than ten opportunities on the entire funnel, and that win only a few number of big sales every year, the exercise might be reasonable to do and certainly worthwhile.

Summary of Traditional Funnel

The inherent flaw of a traditional funnel is defining the funnel stages by selling activity. At best, it doesn't help you. At worst, it misleads you in performing the two functions of a funnel. Is it a guarantee of failure? Of course not. Most of my clients are very successful companies that do a lot of things right. They've used a traditional funnel before they met me. To their credit, they're always trying to find better ways of doing things. They see now that a traditional sales funnel is not a contributor to their success. They've found the BuyCycle Funnel™ to be better. You can too. Let's see how in Part Two, and learn why this better design should be your new standard for funnel management.

Part Two:

A New Standard in Funnel Management

Chapter 3

The BuyCycle Funnel™

So far, we've defined the funnel, explained its two main functions, presented the traditional way of designing and managing the funnel, and shown why it's not ideal. Like my mother would say whenever she heard someone in our house complaining, *"Don't complain unless you've got a better idea."* My better idea is called the BuyCycle Funnel™.

The BuyCycle Funnel™ performs the same two functions as the traditional funnel. That is, it helps you track the journey of a sales opportunity from discovery to close. And, two it helps you manage all opportunities – and answer that important question, "What is my funnel's ability right now to close enough business to hit my quota for the year?" Like a traditional funnel, the BuyCycle Funnel™ has stages. Each stage describes where an opportunity is in its journey toward becoming an order. Here's where the differences become significant.

Based on the Customer's Buying Process

The difference between a traditional funnel and a BuyCycle Funnel™ is in how the funnel stages are defined. We know that in a traditional funnel the definitions are based on selling activity, such as 'leave a sample', 'do a demo', or 'deliver a proposal.' With the BuyCycle Funnel™, the stages are defined by the *customer buying process*, which is the series of stages a customer goes through when the customer makes a purchase. It's a more effective approach to selling and managing your funnel. Let's see exactly how the BuyCycle guides you to sell this way.

Though you'll likely need a custom BuyCycle Funnel™ for your company, first we start with a BuyCycle Funnel™ template that looks like this:

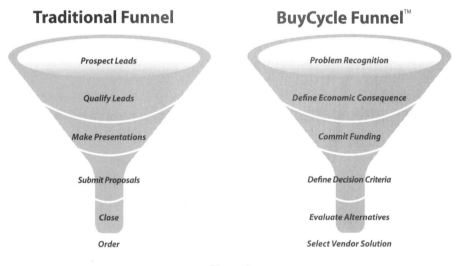

Traditional Funnel

Prospect Leads

Qualify Leads

Make Presentations

Submit Proposals

Close

Order

BuyCycle Funnel™

Problem Recognition

Define Economic Consequence

Commit Funding

Define Decision Criteria

Evaluate Alternatives

Select Vendor Solution

Figure 9

Remember that when the customer makes a purchase, the buying process is done. And, when you've made a sale, the opportunity is no longer on your funnel. Let's look at these stages one-by-one.

Problem Recognition

Unless a customer recognizes a problem (or opportunity) it's going to be hard to sell him or her something. As it should be. You shouldn't sell your products or services to someone if you didn't think you were solving a problem. As a salesperson, your primary responsibility to customers is to help them solve problems or help them realize new opportunities. Some sales people think of this as the pain a customer has. Some of my clients call it a gap in performance. Sometimes, these problems are crystal clear. Sometimes, the problems are not so clear. What looks like a problem is really a symptom of a problem. Maybe you and your contact are both working toward a better understanding of the situation. The bottom line is you need some person at the account to not be completely satisfied with his or her current situation – and your products or services have to address them.

> **It's not a problem until the customer says it is.**

Though Problem Recognition might seem to need no explanation, I see salespeople making mistakes at this stage. Here's a simple rule: *It's not a problem until the customer says so.* It's good sales behavior to be looking for problems. Maybe you'll discover something the customer hasn't seen or realized yet and you make them aware of it. Your intentions are good. But, unless the customer looks you in the eye and says, *"That situation's not acceptable,"* there's no problem recognized and no momentum toward a purchase - and no sales opportunity yet for you.

For example, a client of mine, I'll call her Sarah, sells asset management products to banks like Wachovia and to brokerage companies like Merrill Lynch and UBS. At one of the brokerage houses she called on an analyst whenever she was in the area. He always took time to meet her. This went on for a couple of years. And, while they did talk business during these meetings the analyst never bought a product from my client. He never told her he had any problems. Whenever she and I discussed the account she always said the company had areas where she knew it could use her products such as an underperforming high yield fund or a fund with expenses too high. Unfortunately, he didn't see it that way. Until that changes, he's not likely to buy anything from her. There's no Problem Recognition.

There's nothing complicated about this, but salespeople still make assumptions about customer needs. A lot of it has to do with perception of need - the salesperson's versus the customer's. I won't say yours doesn't count, but I think you know what I mean and which one holds the weight. You've got to get your contact to actually verbalize the problem. And, if you can, to verbalize it more than once. The more they hear themselves state the problem the more they convince themselves there is one, and the closer they come to doing something about it.

Since Problem Recognition comes at an early stage of the buying process, you can't be surprised if your search for problems comes up empty, right? Not every door you knock on will open wide and be full of sales opportunities for a nice, hard-working salesperson like yourself. To get the contact to express a problem to you, it's good to just get the customer talking about what they use, how they use it and what's their impression of his or her situation. After you've earned the right to ask some questions, you might ask questions like these:

- *Could you tell me how long you've been using this product or doing it this way?*

- *Do you use it for any specific application?*

- *Does it work best in certain conditions? Which ones? How often do these conditions occur? What do you do for other conditions?*

- *What's the main objective for what you want to do here?*

- *How would you describe the way this service works compared to others you've used?*

- *Are you able to link better performance to the use of this service? How? If you can't, how important is it that you are able to?*

- *Has the product or service helped you personally in any way?*

One tactic that some people use on prospects that don't seem to have any problems is to first ask questions that are easy for them to answer, then ask a question that might be harder to answer. For example, asking questions about how the product is used is pretty harmless. Or, how long it's been used. But, when you ask a question where the answer might be more difficult to know, such as measuring or linking performance to this product, you might push back or challenge what the customer tells you. Your intention is to expose a gap to help you and the customer learn more about the situation. This might catch the customer off-guard a little, so you slowly ease your way into that line of questioning.

While it can be anyone in the account expressing a problem, it's almost always better if the person has a lot of influence with others. These people can convince or even force others to do certain things. The faster you determine this influence and authority the better you'll qualify early opportunities and set better sales strategy.

Problems Aren't Limited to 'Business' Needs

Let's go back to the gap in performance or pain for just a second. You might have done what most people do when I mentioned gap or pain. You thought of a problem affecting the *business* or the *company*, like productivity or lower sales or higher costs or longer time to market. For sure, those are problem areas you have to find out about, but did you think that the gap or pain could be related to something personal with the person you're talking to? It very much can be. In fact the inspiration for change is often rooted in something personal, not in something affecting the business. Let me give you an example.

A client of mine was promoted to director of sales for a small engineering services company. One of the first things he recognized was the lack of a sales process. He hired me to help him fix that. While the lack of a sales process could affect sales or market share, it also is an opportunity for the director to develop his people and be seen as a strong leader by his people and his boss. If he's successful at growing sales, he meets a business objective, but also satisfies a personal motivation such as recognition, being seen as a leader, earning more influence in the entire company or some other motivation. His salespeople had never had training or strategy in sales process like we provided and they took to it favorably. The director was seen as taking an interest in his people that his predecessor had not. If you appeal to the personal motivation of the customer's buying process, you're more likely to uncover and understand problems.

In the business world, for someone to purchase something, it's almost always necessary (though not always sufficient) to first prove some return on the cost of the purchase, or, at least, make a decent business case that shows the purchase will impact some part of the business measurably. That leads us to the next stage of the customer's buying process.

Define Economic Consequence

While it's almost always necessary to prove some financial benefit of making a purchase, it's not always sufficient. Let me show you what I mean.

A client of mine sells an industrial laundry product and service to nursing homes and health centers. One of the problems these facilities have is keeping their energy costs in control due to all of the hot water they use in cleaning. My client has a product that helps control hot water use and therefore reduces energy costs. They've got the evidence to prove that it works. During a new sales opportunity, the salespeople collect information from the prospect about its existing laundry facility and energy use. Then, they plug that information into a spreadsheet and formula that tells the prospect what kind of savings they can expect. The savings is often impressive and always much more than the cost of purchasing the system.

While you'd think that my client would be making sales every week they're struggling to sell this product. Why?

While the reasons are unique to each opportunity, in general we've learned the following:

- My client isn't always talking to the person who authorizes money to be spent on this purchase.

- My client's sale is competing against other possible purchases.

- The customer thinks that improving other parts of the operation and workflow might generate savings without making another sizeable purchase.

- He is talking to the right person but there's no personal motivation for that person to authorize spending money for this purchase – or, there is personal motivation to *not* take action to spend money for this purchase.

Knowing these reasons might not ease the sting of not advancing a sale but at least they get to the bottom of the client's decision-making motivation. This lets the salesperson adjust his approach and strategy. He might conclude faster too that a prospect is highly unlikely to change and is a waste of time for now.

> **Customers often choose to live with the problems.**

Choosing to Live With the Problem

What's basically happening when a customer expresses a problem but doesn't do anything about it is the customer is choosing to live with the problem. This is not so unusual for several reasons.

One, not all problems are significant. While you'd like to think some are, especially those that could help you gain traction toward a sale, it's not reality. And if it's not significant, then it might not get much attention. A client of mine in Canada that sells a software product struggles at times to convince customers that their 'broken' systems are worth fixing. My client's sale might be a few hundred thousand dollars but the CFO is dealing with multi-million dollar problems every day. It's the same issue with an appliance manufacturer selling washers and dryers and ranges and microwaves and refrigerators to a home builder. The cost of appliances as a percentage of the overall cost to build a house is small, often less than 1%. It doesn't hit the builder's radar screen like the cost of labor, lumber, concrete, windows, cabinets or other items.

Two, there's not enough time in a day to fix every problem. A client of mine said it this way: if all he did was fix problems all day he wouldn't get anything done. We both laughed at the paradox, but we also knew what he was saying. Executives have to pick their battles. Some problems will have higher payoff than others and some might be perceived that way. The question you want to ask is, "Is the customer coming to that conclusion with my help or without it?"

Three, change is a big deal. Even when there's an acknowledged better way to do something and the cost is covered by the benefit, sometimes people will choose to do nothing about it. As a salesperson, you could tackle this inertia with rational arguments all day and waste your time – and that of the customer's. This is not a rational position. It's an emotional one. The customer who lives with the acknowledged problem is saying it's not worth my effort, there's not enough in it for me. He could be afraid of making a change. Until this changes, either voluntarily by the contact or by the contact's boss forcing the change, there's no momentum toward the purchase.

Four, sometimes there really isn't money to be found to fix the problem. It doesn't grow on trees, right? But, I advise my clients to not get sidetracked initially by this speed bump because if a problem is really worth fixing the right person will find money for the purchase. The key to this though is to find the right person – he or she who has the authority to find money to make a purchase eventually. You could spend way too much time with others who don't have this authority and mislead yourself.

Commit Funding

While some problems never get fixed, others do. For that to happen someone's got to commit time and effort to fixing it. And when time and effort alone isn't enough, they also commit money. This leads to the next stage in the customer's buying process, Commit Funding. This stage is one of the most important ones to understand because of its effect on all things related to the funnel. Let's focus on the spirit of the definition to help you get the most out of it.

When an opportunity reaches the Commit Funding stage of the buying process, it means that someone has authorized the *possibility* of spending money to fix the problem. This person is likely the only one authorized to spend this money. By committing to the possibility of spending money he or she is publicly saying the following:

> "I've seen or heard enough about the problem, I realize that doing something about it could cost me money and I'm ok with that."

Compare that to opportunities at either of the previous two stages, Recognize Problem and Define Economic Consequence. At Recognize Problem the customer has simply acknowledged a problem exists. He hasn't committed to understanding it further and acting on it. At Define Economic Consequence the customer has expressed a problem and knows something about the cost of that problem to the company. But, she's still choosing to live with it. Maybe because she's not authorized to spend money to fix it, or maybe she's got other problems that are more important and are getting more attention. Nothing's changed. Talk is cheap.

Let's go back to a couple of examples. The client selling the energy-saving laundry product often gets a contact to agree that energy costs are too high. With a little analysis, he can tell them how much they'd save by using his product. But the sale stalls and usually for one of two main reasons. One, the person with the authority to spend money has decided to not spend money because the payoff almost seems too good to be true. They'd rather live with the problem than take a chance on fixing it. Fixing it requires action and spending money and these things put the customer on the spot to be right about his decision. Two, the person with authority to spend the money is unaware of my client's product and service. That is, my client isn't talking directly to this person. From the seller's position he's just isolated a couple of important variables that he can use to set better strategy.

A Big Deal

When you stop to consider what's happened at the Commit Funding stage, it's easy to see what a big deal it is for an opportunity to make it this far.

Money has now been allocated. Although a check hasn't been written, there's money that's either physically put aside or mentally put aside for this situation. Even if it was budgeted it's still a big deal to spend it. For example, two of my larger clients go through a predictable cycle each year around late summer and early fall where they scrutinize every expense and cut back where it's not deemed necessary even if money has been budgeted for certain expenses. This is intended to positively affect earnings going into year-end.

Someone is publicly defending the decision to spend company funds. This responsibility isn't taken lightly. Before money is spent at a company there needs to be some rationale or a business case for doing so. It could be informal in some companies and could be extremely disciplined in others. Credibility is now on the line. Is the investment going to give a good return? Will it accomplish the objectives? Some people even use the decision as a way to take shots at their perceived enemies and fight political battles within the company.

Other projects that come across his or her desk for evaluation now must compete with this funded project. The flip side of money being allocated for one project is that money might not be available for other projects that come up. A choice has been made. People whose project got bumped down the list or knocked off completely won't be too happy about this.

Someone is publicly stating that how things are done now is not acceptable. A new battle is being waged. This one is very interesting. Not every decision is one that pits one person against another, but for significant decisions it's reasonable that that's exactly what occurs. For example, if a new senior vice president completely restructures the new department he inherits and chooses to make significant investments in CRM software the outgoing VP of this department might look a little foolish – why didn't he make these changes and investments? If the head of IT is an important person in bringing on this new software how does it make her look? She might be thrilled that the investment is finally being made. Or, she might feel it does nothing but increase her workload unnecessarily.

Budgeted Versus Funding Committed

It's tempting to confuse budgeted with Commit Funding.

> **Budgeted is not the same as funding committed.**

Each year many businesses go through a budget process. They determine what they're prepared to spend on various areas to run the business, take care of their employees, and achieve its objectives. However, just because something is budgeted doesn't mean that money will in fact be spent on that.

For example, in our line of work companies might budget for training. They might have no idea what training needs they'll have at the time they budget. They may go through the year and never spend the budgeted dollars on training. If there's no recognized need, there's no perceived need to change and spend budgeted dollars. But, if the customer recognizes a problem and defines its economic consequence he might conclude that the problem is worth addressing. And, addressing it could cost money. Funding is committed.

Another way to look at this is to look at situations where the company would not likely ever have a line item in the budget for a particular product or service. One of my clients sells a software product to multi-site retailers and national restaurant chains. These companies are opening new stores throughout the year as they expand. Once they decide to build a new store location they need many disciplines to work together such as site surveying and engineering, construction and design. There are many different suppliers and contractors involved. There's a need for clear communication throughout the process. My client's software helps these parties do just that. It's like a portal for all important information regarding the construction, design and engineering of each new location.

The companies that buy this software almost never have a line item in their budgets for it. They simply communicate using other means such as email, the telephone, even courier services to send documents. It takes someone to recognize the inefficiency of communicating this way to get the ball rolling for a possible sale for my client and its software solution. And, before it passes the critical stage of Commit Funding the right person will have to step up and authorize getting money somewhere to possibly purchase something that was never budgeted.

Define Decision Criteria

Now that there's a green light given to the possibility of changing and spending money to do so, the next important task in the buying process is to define the criteria for making the decision.

What criteria are we talking about? There's the obvious stuff that you would expect to find under the category of business needs and requirements. Size, shape, color, application, quantity, timing of installation and more. All of that should arise from the discussions of what's not working 100% right for the customer right now. But hasn't that been done already in the customer's buying process? In a way, some of it has and it's likely that some of it has not. What happens at Define Decision Criteria stage is a finalization of this activity.

Early in the buying process at Problem Recognition it's reasonable that someone identified a gap in performance and has formed some opinions about what the problem is and what is necessary to fix it. For example, an influential nurse at a hospital neonatal intensive care unit who is not 100% happy with the way her infusion pumps work may know a fair amount about why they don't work well. After all, she uses them every day. Maybe they're difficult to program or to troubleshoot. Maybe they don't accept a certain size syringe for some types of treatment. If the people in her unit have formed a committee to evaluate current infusion pumps and to consider the purchase of new ones, and she's on that committee, then her opinions about the current pumps would likely be part of the decision criteria. All of the needs and opinions expressed by all of the people participating in the buying process contribute to the decision criteria that will be used to evaluate new pumps. So it is with other products and services that make up the company's buying process for the things they buy.

Who Participates in the Buying Process

In most situations, there will be a group of people who are assigned to participate in the process. Their expertise or experience adds a lot to the task. They might be asked to speak on behalf of their departments. Each one of them brings his or her own thoughts and opinions and biases to the task. Sometimes companies use outside consultants to help with the entire buying process. And, sometimes, they have RFPs (request for proposal) or RFQs (request for quote) written.

Formal or Informal Criteria

Keep in mind that companies don't always go about the buying process in an orderly fashion. It could be due to the purchase being small. It could be due to their not being well-managed. It's the salesperson's job to get inside the company's buying process to get in the best position to win the sale. I can't really say that selling into a formal process is better than selling into an informal one because every sale is unique. However, what you want to do is be able to influence that process and criteria as much as you can.

Sometimes it looks like the customer has reached the Define Decision Criteria stage but it has not. Let me give you an example.

A client of mine is a global energy management firm that sells its services to big box retailers around the world. Their sales are usually several hundred thousand to several million dollars in size and have multi-year contract terms. What they impact gets lots of attention from CFOs and other senior executives due to rising energy costs. In their sale, it's common for their customer to want to go through a fairly thorough business case before any money gets committed to purchase from my client or any other firm. With or without my client's help, the customer goes through that exercise and then knows better what the ROI would need to be to invest time and money in an energy-savings purchase. If they decide to go through with a purchase, then much of their criteria is already set. However, they might have more to learn about their criteria once they engage some firms in their buying process.

Evaluate Alternatives

With the decision criteria set, the customer now advances to a stage of the buying process called Evaluate Alternatives.

The job here is to match the best solution to the company's decision criteria (needs). It should be a lot easier to do that when the criteria are clearly defined. Keep in mind that we're looking for the best solution that meets the defined criteria. If the criteria are not well defined, the company might get an inferior solution. If the criteria do not favor your products or services, then your solution won't stand up as well against other solutions. The better you can help the customer define the decision criteria the better you can see that it matches your solution.

> **If you discover an opportunity late in the customer's buying process, you'll more likely need to discount the price to earn the business.**

For example, if you find out about an opportunity late in the customer's buying process you might have little or no influence on the criteria. The executives have gone through Problem Recognition, Define Economic Consequence and Commit Funding entirely on their own, or with another vendor you compete against. You get called in to bid on the opportunity simply as 'proposal fodder' as one of my clients calls it. You really have little chance at winning this kind of opportunity - but the company needs you to compete. They might need to seek alternative bids to the one they really want. Or, they use you to keep the chosen vendor honest with price and cost. Because they need you to bid you might have more leverage in the sale than you think. The worst thing you can do is aggressively bid on a sale like this when you have a very low likelihood of winning, or aggressively discounting and offering free this and that and incentives everywhere. You give away your value proposition and earned market position when you sell this way; and in this sale, you walk away with nothing in return. This approach will come back to haunt you later when you have a future chance to sell to this customer.

This is one of the best uses of the BuyCycle Funnel™. It helps you see clearly when these situations occur and prevents you from getting so excited about these late-stage opportunities that fly in from nowhere at the last minute. You can still decide to engage if you like, and you might want to do so. You might engage to get access to key people you've been wanting to see or begin developing relationships with key executives that might help you for a future sale. But you have to be careful to not invest too much selling time in these deals.

Select Vendor Solution

After the evaluation stage the customer makes a decision. Sometimes it is one man, one vote and the majority wins. At other times it has to be unanimous. Or, there might be one person who has the ability to veto all others if he or she chooses to. The job of the seller is to know these facts about the buying process for each sale – it leads to better sales strategy.

Although the person with authority to commit the funds might be able to veto all others at this stage it's not routinely done. His veto will usually appear earlier when funding is being considered. Good leaders give their people boundaries to work within and then let them decide what is best. But again it's his veto power to use as he wishes.

I recall a story in our local paper that demonstrates this veto power. A university president asked his board to consider granting tenure to a professor, which was the normal process followed. The board came back and said, "No, tenure shouldn't be granted." The president vetoed the board's decision and granted tenure. This sent shockwaves through the university. This had not been done before. But, it was his right to exercise. And, he did.

The selection can come in the form of a verbal approval or what I call a 'verbal congratulations.' The winning company is told of the good news. It's exciting, but the customer hasn't purchased just yet. There might be negotiations of terms or conditions or delivery schedules or shipping to be defined. Usually it's the seller's deal to lose at this point. Once all of that is agreed on, the next step is a purchase order or contract is signed and a deal is made.

A Key BuyCycle Funnel™ Characteristic – Customer Commitment

There's one characteristic of the BuyCycle Funnel™ that is inherent throughout the customer's buying process – it is *customer commitment*.

> **Each stage of the BuyCycle Funnel™ is defined by customer commitment, because making commitments is inherent in how a customer goes about making a purchase decision.**

In a traditional funnel design, you might see the stage 'do a product demo.' That means that in your selling efforts you're trying to get the customer to allow you to do a demo. You do this because you believe it gets you closer to the sale. That's fine. The only problem is, this commitment is yours, not the customer's. You're the one spending all the energy – and money – doing the demo. You might have to travel, buy a ticket and a hotel room, incur meal expense, get a taxi, etc. Not to mention the opportunity cost of a day-plus of travel and demo time.

To shift from a *selling activity* definition to a *buying process* definition we could ask the following question: "If we do a demo, what is the customer ready and willing to commit to?" I understand that commitment could be different things for each customer. However, usually a demo is done earlier in the sale to generate interest in a product or to explain how something works. Thinking ahead in the process, if the demo is successful in generating interest and answering some usage or application questions, what would the customer typically be prepared to commit to next? The point is, you should be asking this before you do the demo. For some customers, the answer is to learn more about how the product works in their environment. Or it might be to build a better business case for ultimately making the change. As the seller you might ask the prospect to commit manpower and access to making that happen. You might seek a commitment for providing more detailed information that the prospect wouldn't be quick to share unless it was fairly serious about making a change.

Doing demos and product evaluations and sampling product is one area of the sale where the BuyCycle Funnel™ can have a huge impact on sales success and productivity. Another area is delivering proposals.

When a salesperson hears a customer say, "I'd like a proposal," it's easy for the mind to start racing. Proposals *appear* to be a huge milestone in the selling process because a sale *appears* to be around the corner. However, as it is with demos and evaluations and product sampling simply delivering a proposal is not a clear enough indicator of where the customer is in his buying process for the salesperson to make accurate assumptions about buying intention. Let me remind you of the example I shared with you in an earlier chapter.

A client of mine received an RFP and didn't have much access to talk to people at the account. The proposal took several days to prepare – it was worth several hundred million dollars of new business. Though my client had many signs that the customer wasn't committed to working with them my client was too eager to bid on it anyway. They finished the proposal and emailed it. There was no review of the proposal with the customer. Several months after sending it my client still had not heard any response from the customer. Later, they learned they did not get the business. The proposal was their next step in the selling process but they questioned if the customer was genuinely interested in giving them a shot at the business. It's good to know this beforehand.

Why Customer Commitment Matters

The BuyCycle Funnel™, designed with customer commitment, identifies how customers buy and addresses two common and often costly mistakes that sales people make:

- One, not getting commitment from customers during the sale.

- Two, willingly committing to selling activities without getting the customer to commit to something in return.

For example, let's go back to the demo. If you commit to doing a product demonstration the success of the demo can depend on whether or not you have the right people in the room and if they commit to something reasonable as a next step that moves the sale along. These are reasonable demands. Still, I see sales people making their own commitments without getting commitments from the customer for these things. I understand that you don't always get what you ask for. I also understand that when you don't ask, you often don't get.

In another example, the customer may ask you for a proposal. If you agree, but don't demand a proposal review with the right person, then you're setting yourself up for disappointment. A client of mine that sells engineering consulting services routinely prepared and sent proposals by email without requiring any phone or face-to-face review. These proposals often reached six figures. It simply sends the wrong message about your value and your lack of process when you sell this way.

You might take a moment right now to think of a sale or two you're actively working. Use the BuyCycle Funnel™ to validate where the prospects are in their buying process. If you use a traditional funnel, compare it to the BuyCycle Funnel™ by asking yourself a few questions:

- *What do I know about the customer's buying process for this sales opportunity?*

- *How have my selling activities helped the customer commit to taking action on the situation?*

- *What has the customer committed to?*

- *What has the customer not committed to yet?*

- *What can I do now that might help the customer make the next commitment?*

- And, most importantly, what am I prepared to do if the customer refuses to commit to something I ask him to right now, something I believe is very reasonable and appropriate for him to commit to, if he's serious about moving forward?

Why the BuyCycle Funnel™ Will Help You Be More Effective at Selling and Managing Your Sales Funnel

The BuyCycle Funnel™ is a more effective way to perform the two functions of a sales funnel. Let's see how.

Working a Sales Opportunity from Discovery to Close

Using a BuyCycle Funnel™, you can set a better sales strategy to win business. The BuyCycle Funnel™ helps you better understand where the customer is in its intention to making a purchase. You'll be looking for evidence of what the customer has committed to – and hasn't. You'll know better what you know and don't know about customer needs and criteria and who's involved in the purchase decision. You'll have a good idea of what the customer should be willing to commit to next as part of its buying process.

A BuyCycle Funnel™ helps your selling activities have a greater impact. Once you understand where the customer is in its buying process you'll know better what selling activity you should do next. If the customer is prepared to act some way on the demo you do or the sample you provide, then you'll feel confident that this activity will help the customer advance to the next stage. You won't be as likely to do some selling activity that doesn't clearly have an impact. You'll save money, time and many hassles. Your sales productivity will go up. Your close rate will likely increase.

The BuyCycle Funnel™ helps you qualify active interest from passive interest. Active interest is where a customer is committed to taking action on a situation. She's no longer willing to live with the problem. You've got to love these people – without them, you'd have no sales. She may be limited in her authority to spend money, but she may be seen as a thought leader with intelligent ideas. Since taking action is evidence of commitment, when you see it you'll better know what it could mean for your selling efforts.

Managing a sales opportunity using the BuyCycle Funnel™ helps you be more effective and productive by selling to the customer's buying process. It might appear to be a subtle difference from the traditional approach, but becoming a better salesperson is often about finding the small improvements you can make over time that add up to a significant difference in your overall performance.

The BuyCycle Funnel™ also has a big impact on the second function of a funnel, that is managing all of the sales opportunities. Let's see how.

More Accurate Funnel Valuation with the BuyCycle Funnel™

With a funnel full of opportunities at different stages, come Monday morning you've got to decide which ones get your attention, how much of your attention, and your attention first. In other words, you've got to manage your funnel.

But, to put it as simple as I can, what funnel management is really about is working all of these opportunities efficiently for one purpose – to achieve your sales goal by year-end. Therefore, the one question you need to be asking of your funnel in this second function is this:

> **What is my funnel's ability right now to close enough business to hit my quota for the year?**

The BuyCycle Funnel™ gives you a more accurate answer to that question than the traditional funnel. Let's briefly review how the traditional funnel answers the question and why the BuyCycle Funnel™ is a better approach.

Funnel Valuation Using Traditional Funnel

In the previous chapter, I explained three ways to value your funnel using a traditional approach. One, count 100% of the dollar value of every opportunity at every stage. Two, count 100% of the dollar value of the opportunities that reach a certain stage. Three, count a percentage of the dollar value of each opportunity based on the stage of the opportunity. This is a weighted funnel.

The second approach is an effort to improve on the first one, and the third approach is an effort to improve on the second one. But all three have limits.

Every Opportunity Counted Toward Funnel Value

The problem with the first approach is counting toward your funnel value the opportunities that are very early in the customer's buying process. They're so early that even the customer is not likely to know the dollar value of the (purchase) sale. For example, an account manager for an appliance manufacturer might target a home builder that the account manager has never sold to or has not sold to in a very long time. Let's say he knows the builder builds 500 homes a year. He takes the dollar value of the average appliance package he'd sell to the builder and multiplies it by 500 homes and quickly comes up with a rough number of the value of the sales opportunity. However, this can be grossly misleading. For one, the builder might have no intention right now of switching the business from his or her current appliance manufacturer. It's not even a sale at all at this point. Two, if the builder is willing to switch, he might give the account manager a shot at one project, say a 75-home development. That's a far cry from a sale for 500 homes. If this seems too straightforward to state, then why is this mistake made by salespeople all the time? It's the kind of thing that overstates a funnel and gives the salesperson a wrong baseline from which to manage his or her funnel and achieve the sales goal.

Count Some Opportunities Toward Funnel Value

The problem with the second approach goes back to how the funnel stages are defined. When the stages are defined by selling activity you're still setting yourself up for an improper funnel valuation. Let me give you another example.

A region manager for a client of mine counted toward funnel value 100% of the opportunities that his salespeople sent proposals to. This stage was the fourth one on his traditional funnel. At one point he had a region funnel value of $15M, that is, $15M of opportunities that had been quoted. He needed his region to close another $5M in sales to hit the quota.

Unfortunately, several of the proposals should never have been sent – they were never seriously considered by the customer, even though in some cases the customer asked for the proposal. The customer wasn't ready to act on these proposals. Therefore, the $15M funnel value was not accurate. It was misleading the manager and his people to believe their funnel's ability to close enough business right now was better than it really was. If the region needed another $5M of sales to hit its quota, and the region funnel was valued at $15M, you'd be right to believe that this funnel was in pretty good shape. But what if the funnel value was only $5M - how would you feel then? This manager would need his salespeople to close every sale to hit the quota - and that's not likely to happen.

Weighted Funnel

This leads us to the third approach, a weighted funnel. This is where each funnel stage is given a percentage likely to close. The dollar value of the opportunities at each stage is multiplied by the percentage for the stage. You add up the weighted value of all opportunities at all stages to get the overall funnel value. For example, a sales opportunity of $100,000 at a stage that is given a 10% likelihood to close is valued at $10,000. As the opportunity moves down the funnel and closer to a sale it might reach a stage that gets a 50% likelihood. This opportunity would then be valued at $50,000.

So what's wrong with a weighted funnel? Maybe you already guessed it. If the stages are defined by selling activity, then weighting your funnel doesn't overcome the flaws in that model. The other problem with a weighted funnel is putting any dollar value on early stage opportunities. Why should a $500,000 sales opportunity at stage 1 get any funnel value at all, even 10%? These opportunities are almost always too early to know with enough certainty the dollar value of the opportunity. Many of these early stage opportunities are nothing more than the salesperson trying to justify some level of selling activity for his or her funnel. Often, they're comprised of accounts that the salesperson has been chasing for some time with no advancement of an opportunity. It's good to have target accounts, but it's also good to know the difference between a target account and a sales opportunity within it. Counting only a percentage of these early stage deals might seem minor but it's not good practice. It suggests that you've got some back-up plan or safety net covering you in case you don't prospect enough and generate enough new leads. This is wishful thinking.

The final problem with a weighted funnel is that the stage percentages are typically arbitrarily assigned. What makes a stage 1 opportunity 10% likely to close? How is that percentage validated? Going further down the funnel, how do you validate that a stage deserves a 50% likelihood of closing? Even worse, some companies allow the salesperson to assign the percentage likelihood himself. So instead of having one arbitrarily assigned percentage, the company has several. It leads to inconsistencies in funnel valuation and makes forecasting and overall sales coaching extremely difficult.

That said about a weighted funnel, some of my clients value their funnels this way and are convinced that it helps them.

Better Valuation Using the BuyCycle Funnel™

How is the BuyCycle Funnel™ a better way to value your funnel than any of these three above?

One, the BuyCycle Funnel™ **more accurately identifies where the opportunities are in the customer's buying process.** The first step to a correct answer to the *funnel ability* question is having sales opportunities placed on the funnel correctly where they belong. Here, the BuyCycle Funnel™ outperforms the traditional funnel. A selling-activity based funnel places an opportunity on the funnel based on something you the seller have completed, like doing a demo or delivering a proposal. Selling activity is an indicator of your commitment, not the customer's. Just because you've committed to something in your selling process doesn't mean the customer is committed to something in his buying process. The BuyCycle Funnel's stages are defined by customer commitment which is more accurate in describing where the customer is in his buying process.

Two, the BuyCycle Funnel™ **counts toward funnel value only those opportunities that reach the Commit Funding stage.** The second step to valuing the funnel correctly is counting toward funnel value only those deals that have reached a stage where the person with authority to spend says, *"I'm ok with the possibility of spending money to fix these problems."* This occurs at Commit Funding. This isn't the same as making a purchase. It's not the customer saying,*"I'm going to buy from you."* And it's certainly not the customer giving you or any other supplier a blank check. It means he's prepared for the possibility of spending money to fix the problems that have been presented to him, which is a huge milestone to reach in the buying process. At earlier stages, the customer has discovered problems, but has not yet committed to the possibility of spending money. Brian Tracy in his classic book the <u>Psychology of Selling</u> says that if you become one of the 20% of salespeople who produce 80% of the sales, you'll never have to worry about making money again. You can sell. I'll add, if you master the distinction between <u>customer problem</u> and <u>customer commitment to do something about the problem</u>, you'll have a long career in selling.

To see how Commit Funding affects the accuracy of your funnel value, let's look at an example.

In a hypothetical territory with a $5M quota, the sales person has sold $1M so far this year (YTD = year-to-date sales). We'll say this territory uses a five-stage funnel and it has ten opportunities on it. Each opportunity has a dollar value that is based on the salesperson's knowledge of the opportunity. When the dollar value of all ten opportunities is totaled, this funnel has a traditional value of $5M, as seen in the Funnel Dashboard below:

Traditional Funnel

$5,000,000	Quota
$1,000,000	YTD Sales
$4,000,000	Gap
$5,000,000	Funnel Value

But, let's say we learn that six of the ten opportunities have not yet reached the stage where the customer is committed to the possibility of spending money to fix the problems. The dollar value of those six opportunities is $3.75M. Therefore, that leaves four sales opportunities that have reached Commit Funding. The dollar value of those four sales is $1,250,000. The BuyCycle Funnel™ Dashboard looks different, below:

Traditional Funnel

$5,000,000	Quota
$1,000,000	YTD Sales
$4,000,000	Gap
$5,000,000	Funnel Value

BuyCycle Funnel™ Dashboard

$5,000,000	Quota
$1,000,000	YTD Sales
$4,000,000	Gap
$1,250,000	Funnel Value

What does this mean? It means this funnel's true ability to close enough business to hit quota is not as good as it looks. In the misleading traditional funnel, there's $5M of funnel value trying to close $4M of gap. In the BuyCycle Funnel™ there's $1.25M of funnel value trying to close $4M of gap – that's not even close to having enough to close the gap. The salesperson could win all of the opportunities counted toward funnel value on the BuyCycle Funnel™ ($1.25M) and still be far short of closing the gap for the year.

Leads to a Better Way to Spend Your Time

So what? The payoff is in how you spend your time come Monday morning.

> **A BuyCycle Funnel™ helps you be more productive in how you spend your time.**

If you had a funnel like this, and used the traditional funnel to determine how to spend your time, you might be tempted to do little prospecting and instead try to win the deals that make up your $5M funnel. If you use the BuyCycle Funnel™ instead you'd likely spend a lot of time finding new leads since the funnel's ability right now is not good enough to close the gap to hit your quota.

Some BuyCycle Terms to Manage the Process

I'd like to introduce a couple of simple terms to help you use the BuyCycle Funnel™.

Viable Opportunity

When a sales opportunity reaches the Commit Funding stage it's called a Viable Opportunity. It is Viable once the person with authority to spend the money says he or she is ok with spending money. This is a significant milestone to reach in the customer's buying process. Viable means 'sufficiently developed.' Meaning, it is very likely that the company you're trying to sell to will make a purchase from some vendor, though it may not be you. All of the stages from the first Viable stage to the last stage before a purchase are Viable stages.

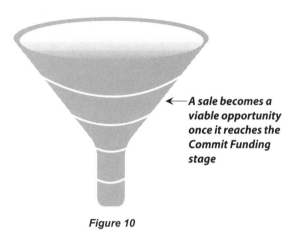

←*A sale becomes a viable opportunity once it reaches the Commit Funding stage*

Figure 10

But why are Commit Funding opportunities Viable and others are not? There's just no way you can say with high confidence <u>and</u> consistency that a sales opportunity that is very early in the buying process will become an order some day for any company. These opportunities have a tremendous distance to travel to become an order. There are many potential obstacles to overcome such as getting funding, competing with other company initiatives, and competition. The key factor, though, goes back to choosing to live with the problem. Companies have lots of problems and executives can't fix every one of them. Many problems never get fixed because they never get funded to be fixed. However, when the person of authority to spend says he's prepared to do so you've got a significant advance in the customer's buying process that can now be quantified.

NonViable Opportunity

A NonViable Opportunity is one that is on the funnel but has yet to reach the first Viable stage of Commit Funding.

Using the BuyCycle Funnel™ template, NonViable stages would be Problem Recognition and Define Economic Consequence.

It's important to remember that the progression is that some NonViables become Viables and some Viables become orders. It's good to know how many NonViables you need to produce one Viable Opportunity. The mission, in a way, is to always have enough NonViable Opportunities that you are actively pursuing because a percentage of these will become Viable Opportunities. Once they become Viables your hit-rate kicks in and you close your historical percentage of Viable Opportunities. Hopefully, it's enough for you to achieve your quota.

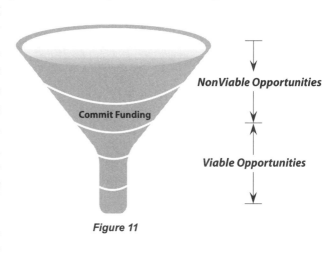

Figure 11

Some funnel models stress A-B-P – Always Be Prospecting. While it's hard to argue with this, it's not the most efficient way to manage your funnel. In some cases, it actually can hurt you. Look at the sample Funnel Dashboard below:

$5,000,000	Quota
$1,000,000	YTD Sales
$4,000,000	Gap
$20,000,000	Funnel Value

This funnel looks like it's rocking. It has five times the dollar value of sales opportunities that is needed to close the GAP to achieve quota. Let's say this is your funnel and you have a close rate of about one third, or 33%. With this funnel you have more than enough opportunities to let that close rate kick in and hit your quota. In fact, with a 33% close rate, you're on track to bringing in $6.6M in new sales, much more than the $4M you need. So, the question is why would you spend a lot of time prospecting when your prospecting has accomplished its objective? Your prospecting has produced for your funnel more than enough Viable Opportunities for your hit rate to kick in and achieve your quota.

But, what if some of those Viable Opportunities don't close? Well, you know right now that some of them won't close. In fact, according to your hit rate about two thirds of them won't close. But you don't need all of them to close, do you? If you ever have a funnel like this you're better off spending most of your time trying to win the Viable Opportunities that you've successfully qualified. Let your close rate take over and watch the sales come in.

If you're concerned about staying busy with a funnel like this, then start working next year's funnel right now. A client of mine the other day told me one of his reps was 125% on plan for his 2008 funnel – this was August 2007! The only way he could have achieved that is by working his 2008 funnel early in 2007. He's a real pro.

Total Viable Revenue (TVR)

Total Viable Revenue is the dollar value of all of the Viable Opportunities on the funnel at all stages combined. For example, if the first Viable stage is stage 3 and you have a 6-stage funnel, then stages 3 through 6 are all Viable Opportunities and represent Total Viable Revenue. This number is one of the keys to the question, *"What is my funnel's ability right now to close enough business to hit my quota for the year?"* The other key is close rate. You take your close rate, look at GAP and ask yourself if your Total Viable Revenue times close rate is equal to or greater than your GAP. If the answer is, " yes," then your funnel's ability to close enough business to hit quota looks good.

Funnel Factor

Another term the system uses is called Funnel Factor.

Funnel Factor is referred to as a percentage or a whole number. It is how much Total Viable Revenue your funnel has compared to the GAP you have to close to hit your quota. You get Funnel Factor as follows:

> **Total Viable Revenue/GAP = Funnel Factor**

For example, we can calculate funnel factor with the Funnel Dashboard below:

Quota	$5,000,000
YTD Sales	$1,000,000
Gap	$4,000,000
TVR	$1,250,000
Funnel Factor	0.31

At a quick glance, you can see that the funnel is far short of the TVR that it needs to close the GAP and hit quota. With a Funnel Factor less than 1, you could close every Viable Opportunity and still not hit your quota. Closing every Viable Opportunity requires a 100% hit rate. This funnel needs a lot of prospecting.

Let's say you commit to a heavy amount of prospecting and over the next 90 days you have a lot to show for your efforts. Your funnel might change to look like this:

Quota	$5,000,000
YTD Sales	$2,000,000
Gap	$3,000,000
TVR	$3,250,000
Funnel Factor	1.08

You've closed some business and added to TVR. Your funnel has just over a 1:1 ratio of GAP versus TVR. Another way of looking at this Funnel Factor is this. For every dollar you have to close toward hitting quota your funnel has $1.08 worth of Viable Opportunities. On the earlier Funnel Dashboard 90 days ago your funnel had 31 cents of Viable Opportunities for every dollar you needed to close toward hitting quota. You're moving in the right direction.

Benchmark Funnel Factor - What's the Right Funnel Factor to Have?

Though there are no well-known and accepted studies that recommend a target Funnel Factor, it is generally accepted that most businesses start with a factor of 3. That is, the funnel should have three times in sales opportunities the GAP that's left to close to hit quota. However, here are some things to think about as you define the benchmark or target Funnel Factor for your business.

Close Rate

Your benchmark Funnel Factor is determined by your close rate. If your benchmark Funnel Factor is 3 x GAP, then you're saying you close about one-third of all deals you chase. If you say your close rate is 50%, then your benchmark Funnel Factor should be 2 x GAP.

When you're determining close rate, be cognizant of this: at what funnel stage are you saying you have this close rate? For example, if you say that of everything that hits your funnel from the very first stage, you close 25%, then you'd likely have a higher close rate on sales that reach the Commit Funding stage. I recommend starting with Commit Funding to determine your close rate and set your benchmark Funnel Factor from there. It might take a while for you to know your close rate, so starting with a 3 x GAP benchmark is not a bad idea.

Summary of BuyCycle Funnel™

I hope I've been able to shed light on a few things:

1. The BuyCycle Funnel™ is based on the customer's buying process and customer commitment.

2. It is a more effective way of selling and managing the funnel than using a traditional funnel and selling activities because it more accurately places the sales opportunities where they belong on the funnel.

3. Selling activities have a greater impact when they are well-timed to the customer's buying process.

4. The BuyCycle Funnel™ encourages the salesperson to constantly seek customer commitment throughout the buying process.

5. The BuyCycle Funnel™ gives you good funnel data which is critical to accurately valuing your funnel and knowing your chances of achieving quota for the year.

6. Accurate funnel valuation helps you make good decisions on how to spend your time to work your funnel.

Having a BuyCycle Funnel™ can make a big difference in your sales performance, one sale at a time and in helping you manage your funnel effectively. The focus of this chapter has been on presenting the rationale for a BuyCycle Funnel™ approach over the traditional approach, why it's more effective and how it works.

The key to getting a payoff from using the BuyCycle Funnel™ is to adopt it as a fundamental, disciplined selling approach. This will likely require a new commitment on your part to a new funnel process. Let's see why process is a key to maximum gain with the BuyCycle and how you can create a BuyCycle Funnel™ process yourself.

Chapter 4

The Basis for a Buying Cycle-based Funnel Model

While the idea of a buying process model for selling is not something I created, applying it to the funnel is an innovative and effective way to combine the two functions of selling and managing the funnel function. In the spirit of being a student of the craft, you'll want to know more about this concept of a buying process, who made it popular, what research has been done in it, and how it has been applied to the field of selling. The more you know about it, the better you'll understand how the BuyCycle Funnel™ works and how you can use it to be more successful selling.

In a way, the BuyCycle Funnel™ is another expression of the study of buyer behavior that has been going on for nearly 40 years.

A Buying Process or a Selling Process?

To understand the idea of a buying process let's compare it to what's common in the field of selling, a selling process.

A *buying process* is the series of steps or milestones that collectively defines how a purchase is made. That could be an individual purchase or a purchase made by a group of individuals at a company. A *selling process* is a series of steps defined by selling activities that describes the things a salesperson does to move a sale from lead discovery to a closed sale. A typical series of activities is outlined in the last chapter. In a way, you're involved in both a selling and buying process when you sell. But the emphasis is usually far too heavy on the selling process side. The difference is significant - let me tell you how one client experienced it.

The client was a VP of Sales of a division of a large industrial products company that sold products to a variety of industries and customers. The VP was taking his new salesperson in to see the purchasing agent of a large auto supplier. This supplier was an account they had sold to for years and the purchasing agent was an old friend of the VP's. With the former salesperson leaving, coverage of the account had been spotty. The VP wanted to show the purchasing agent that he was committed to the account. On this visit, the VP was actually expecting to take an order since the company was scheduled to make a purchase according to the VP's sales records.

When they got to the purchasing agent's office, the agent reluctantly agreed to see them. The VP explained that he was helping the new salesperson get introduced to the important people in the account. The agent said he no longer had his old job – it was eliminated recently in a restructuring. Not only could he not place orders with the VP's company as he had done before, he had to tell the VP that the VP's business was going out to bid. It wasn't the agent's decision, though he played a part by participating in the new purchasing committee. A new director of the department decided to change the company's purchasing policies. The VP and his salesperson left the plant scrambling to recover and come up with a way to save the business. The VP said to me, *"They no longer buy from us the way we want to sell to them."* Well put. I would say that the buying process had changed.

It's bad enough for this salesperson inheriting an account that once was a key customer that bought lots of stuff and now was threatening to leave. Unfortunately for the VP, his salesforce had a long list of customers just like this one - companies that were undergoing changes in the way they sourced product.

But the salesforce was deeply conditioned to sell a certain way, and that way was a focus on selling activity. They pitched the product, told customers why they should buy it, and justified the product's higher price as 'value add'. They even packaged a couple of products together and called it a 'solution'. The VP's salesforce scrambled to rescue falling sales in the months to come. It increased its average daily call activity. They did more product training. They modified the offering. Eventually, sales dropped so much that the company reorganized the salesforce altogether. It went from having four separate, specialty salesforces selling a limited line of products to one larger sales force that carried the full line of products. While it made sense to give salespeople more products to sell to the same customers, it did not get to the root cause of the problem – a salesforce that was still conditioned to sell how it wanted to sell, not how its customers wanted to buy. They'll continue to struggle until they figure this out and make necessary changes.

When selling activity is the focus, getting to the next step of the selling process is the goal. This focus can not only blind you to discovering the customer's real needs, it can also lead to making many assumptions about the people involved in the purchase. But just because someone was involved in a past purchase in a certain way doesn't mean he or she will be involved in a current purchase in the same way, or be involved at all.

A buying process based selling approach helps you effectively deploy your selling activities. With a buying process focus, your first task is to know where the customer is in its decision-making process. Then, you decide what selling activities have the biggest impact on moving the sale along – that is, moving the customer along its buying process. For example, instead of sending a proposal because it's the next step in your selling process, you'd prepare it and require a proposal review when the customer gives you strong reason to believe he or she is ready to act on it. Instead of offering a free trial or evaluation or free samples, you should confirm that the customer is ready to use those samples to move toward making a purchase or use the evaluation results to do the same. The customer should show signs of committing to something in return for the sampling or evaluation activity – something that will make the sample or the trial even more valuable to the customer – and will get you closer to a sale. This sequence - knowing where the customer is in the buying process and selecting the right selling activity - keeps you focused on the customer and enables you to sell more effectively.

The study of a buying process approach to selling has been researched and reported on for several decades. Let's review some models of the buying process for individuals.

The EKB Model

One of the pioneers of research in the area of individual decision-making is Roger Blackwell, a former professor of marketing at The Ohio State University.

In 1968, Blackwell teamed with two other professors to create the EKB model of consumer behavior. That model, named after its three authors, explained how individuals go about the decision making process when purchasing consumer goods. The model is below:

Inputs	Information Processing	Decision Processing	D.P. Variables	External Factors
Stimuli of Marketers and Others	Exposure	Problem Recognition	Beliefs	Cultural Norms
	Attention	Search	Attitudes	
	Yielding/ Acceptance	Alternative Evaluation	Intentions	Group Influence
	Retention	Choice	Evaluation Criteria	Family Influence
		Outcomes	Lifestyle	
	Comprehension	Satisfaction/ Dissatisfaction	Normative Compliance	Unexpected Circumstances

MEMORY

The EKB model revealed that many factors are involved in making purchasing decisions, including psychological factors, memory, evaluation of basic needs, subconscious stimuli and more. Using EKB to explain the purchase of a new set of golf clubs, the decision process might go something like this.

Problem Recognition:

The buying process starts when the golfer recognizes a problem. Something triggers his awareness of not being 100% satisfied with his game (maybe it's losing money every weekend to his buddies). He might think it's a problem with his putter. He might have good days and bad days with it. After a bad day, he might be ready to break it in two. After a good day, he quickly forgets and does nothing about it.

Information Search:

At this stage, the golfer is motivated to look into the situation further and seek more information. He may try to correct the problem by taking a lesson or practicing more. He may seek advice from playing partners or a friend. He might buy a golf magazine. The more he searches, the more his awareness is heightened. He might begin to notice ads for golf clubs or check out what putters other people are using. He might notice a golf club store while out running an errand. He might even purposely visit that store and play around with the putters on its practice area.

Evaluation and Choice

At this stage, the golfer has made up his mind that something needs to be done about the current putter he's using – it needs to be replaced. He may go to a golf store or his golf course and experiment with putters. He may try one that his friend uses. He forms preferences about style, brand, design, and price.

Choice

The golfer has decided which putter to buy. He knows where he could buy it, considers location and price, and reputation, and is now ready to purchase.

Outcomes

In Outcome, he buys the putter.

Satisfaction/Dissatisfaction

EKB includes a stage that is post-purchase. Here, the golfer evaluates his level of satisfaction about the decision he made. For the purchase of a putter, I'm sure he's expecting to make more putts and win back those lost bets from his buddies. In this step he puts closure to the entire process that began when he recognized his game was not what he wanted it to be.

The Value to Sales and Marketing

You can quickly see how a model like this would be of great value to sales and marketing departments. Understanding how to influence a person's purchase behavior can help you market and sell more effectively. Marketers can design promotions or advertising to have an impact on a specific part of the customer's buying process. For example, if the seller felt that the target customer needed to be better-educated on an application before they could be expected to buy, the seller could target that.

One of my clients, a healthcare company that sells products to hospitals and clinics, is doing this right now to change the perception its customers have of the problems that hospitals face regarding patient care, and their perception of the right way to approach those problems. Their marketplace is pretty much divided into two camps, one that buys the cheaper solutions that aren't as effective and have to be used more often, and one that buys the higher priced, clinically superior solutions that are more effective and provide a longer effect.

My client is seen by its marketplace as the clinically superior choice and the higher priced solution.   The problem is that a higher priced solution is perceived as more <u>costly</u> to the hospital, but that's not necessarily true.   In fact, if the customers used my client's higher priced solutions exactly as they're intended they'd save money on the overall goal, the cost of treating patients.

The Buying Process of Groups

While much of the research on customer buying process is about how individuals make purchase decisions for themselves, there is also research on how individuals make decisions when working as part of a group of people coming together to make a purchase, such as in the business to business world. Before we look at that research let's take a moment to compare buying process for an individual and buying process for a group of people.

If you're an individual you have only one person to please - yourself.

- Regarding *timing*, it's up to you to decide when to buy.

- You set *the budget* for the purchase and you approve funds.

- You *define all of the criteria*. It must meet your needs and that's all that matters.

- If you make a wrong choice you're the one who has to live with it.

EKB tells us that you're likely influenced by many variables, including other people such as your friends and colleagues and family members. You could feel pressure to make a statement with work colleagues or neighbors. But it's still just you making the decision.

On the other hand, being a part of the group of decision makers is a different story.

You're one of several people participating in the decision. You're not the only one whose needs need to be satisfied. You have to work together on problem recognition, scope of problem, identifying solutions, and perhaps implementation after purchase. No one says you have to play nice with others, but you do have to play with them.

You have a distinct role to play. That's why you're on the team. You might be brought in because you have a lot of knowledge of the application or the product. You might be a consensus builder. You might be representing your department or your staff and its needs. You might have excellent project management skills. Whatever the reason is, you are part of the buying process and you're expected to play a role in it.

The timing for making the decision is based on several inputs and variables. When people in business get together to buy it can be quite a challenge to get everyone aligned and committed to the same goal. Beyond all of the individual issues like preferences and perceptions of a need to change in the first place, businesses have to allocate money for purchases. It's got to fit into budget parameters or at least be justified if it goes beyond those parameters. It has to meet timing needs. People have to meet throughout the process. The project competes for time with all of the other things people are responsible for.

This purchase competes with other purchases and initiatives. In business, there's always competition for alternate uses of funds. For example, the purchase of a new software system for accounting and finance might compete with the purchase of a new piece of equipment for a part of the manufacturing facility.

You could easily have competing interests and motivations among committee members. Now we're into the politics of the decision. One person on the buying team might be reluctant to switch from whatever product or system is currently in place, maybe because he was responsible for bringing that current system into the company. Replacing it might look unfavorable to his credibility.

Someone else could see this as an opportunity to expose this person's poor decision making earlier – and make a name for herself as the next in line for the promotion. A friend of mine worked for a company that created a job for someone in marketing to move off the shelf millions of dollars of custom made, one of a kind product that in truth had no marketability. The product was overbuilt for customers who no longer wanted or needed it. All of this inventory was carried at an expense. It could have been written off, though it would have resulted in a reported loss. Instead, more resources were used to try to move the unwanted product. Why? Speculation was that someone who was responsible for the extra inventory being built didn't want to get a reputation for poor management skills. Writing off the product could be seen as admitting to a mistake. But as they say, two wrongs don't make a right.

Though there are differences in the dynamics of individual purchasing and purchasing within a group, the similarities in how people go about the buying process are too closely alike. You can benefit a lot from what Blackwell and others have learned. Let's briefly see the research that's been done with group buying processes.

Sheth and Howard

Another pioneer in the field of decision making processes was Jagdish Sheth, also a professor, now at the Goizueta School of Business at Emory University in Atlanta. Sheth was a doctoral student in the 1960's studying under a professor named John Howard. In 1969 Sheth and Howard published a book called Theory of Buyer Behavior. This work laid an important foundation for the field of consumer behavior and marketing. In 1973 Sheth published a paper called "A Model of Industrial Buyer Behavior". He subsequently published many books and over 200 articles on marketing related topics. The field of this study was starting to take off.

Formalizing a Process for Selling

There must be something in the water at universities because in 1982 another marketing professor published an article in the Harvard

Business Review called <u>Major Sales: Who Really Does the Buying?</u> This Harvard professor was Thomas Bonoma. In the paper, Bonoma referred to a *buying center and roles* which sellers could use to greatly improve their understanding of a customer's buying process. Bonoma gave credit in the paper to a 1972 work by Frederick Webster Jr. and Yoram Wind in work they published called <u>Organizational Buying Behavior</u>. Bonoma suggested that Webster and Wind were the first to publish the idea of a buying center that exists when groups of individuals come together to make a purchase such as in a business to business environment.

Bonoma's paper was groundbreaking because he talked about the science of the buying process not in academic terms, but rather in a more approachable fashion. It made a lot of sense for example to think of the decision making process in terms of several people involved and the different roles they played in the purchase. In one role a person *proposes* to replace an existing supplier or product. In another role, a person *evaluates* different suppliers to consider. In a third role, a person who *uses* the product everyday comments on how well it works and what might be improved. Bonoma also suggested that using psychology can improve selling effectiveness. For example, he says that the CEO or business owner who buys a corporate jet could be fulfilling a lifelong dream that began as a young boy, almost a promise if you will of buying that jet when he makes it to the top. As a seller if you understand even at a surface level the CEO's personal motivations you could tailor your sales strategy to meet his real needs and win him over. You're likely to be differentiated by this CEO among other sellers who don't recognize and sell to this personal motivation.

Finally, Bonoma's paper came at a time when corporate purchasing was becoming more complex and made selling more challenging. Bonoma's approach helped a salesperson understand the buying process better, reduce some of the complexity of the sale, and set better strategies.

Commercial Success of a Formalized Sales Approach

Bonoma's work never translated into commercial success for him in the form of becoming a guru for sales process or sales training, and I suspect that he didn't try to pursue that path anyway. But something like his work did become commercially successful for two other men by the name of Steve Heiman and Robert B. Miller.

Miller and Heiman popularized the idea of a buying center that Bonoma published in his Harvard Business Review paper. They did this in their best selling book <u>Strategic Selling</u> (1985 Warner Books). This book was groundbreaking for several reasons. One, it was aimed directly at salespeople and designed to help them sell in a complex environment. Two, the method was simple to understand and use. Three, they assembled several key concepts surrounding the buying center idea, formalized and simplified the approach and therefore made it accessible to the huge audience of sales people. These concepts include psychology of the buyers, whether or not a buyer favors your solution or a different one, roles, defining the sale scope, and more. They deserve much credit for simplifying and organizing the concepts that others were researching and writing about. Today, the Miller Heiman company is a global sales training leader and Strategic Selling is one of the most popular and effective sales courses used.

Two Roads Diverged and… They Took the Selling Process Path

Strategic Selling accomplished what other respectable, well known sales methods also accomplished. Putting a structure to the selling process that is easy to understand and to use. The value of this cannot be overstated. While there are a good handful of these courses, three others that are worth noting are Solution Selling, Counselor Selling and SPIN Selling. They've made a huge impact on salesforce skill development and sales performance.

However, despite their success and effectiveness, these courses are still not pure buying process based. They don't first and foremost direct the seller to understand the customer's buying process before setting sales strategy. The methods do a good job of helping salespeople understand customer needs and motivations and how to ask questions and get commitment and to see how individuals relate to one another in the purchase decision. That's more than ok – it's critical to good selling. But in the spirit of continuous improvement in sales methods, what's needed is ironically a model that goes back to the spirit of the original research of Sheth and Howard and Blackwell into how people and groups of people go through a buying process. The BuyCycle Funnel™ is intended to be that model.

I hope you've drawn the next conclusion.

> **Combining the BuyCycle Funnel™ with any of these selling methods above or with any one of several other excellent methods on the market today is a powerful combination.**

The BuyCycle Funnel™ helps the seller focus on the customer decision making process while these customer facing selling methods provide effective ways of doing discovery, selling within a group of people, getting commitment, building trust, and more. The BuyCycle makes these other selling methods more powerful than each one is by itself. In a later chapter you'll learn more about how to combine these two into a sales process for your company.

But – wait just a minute. While the BuyCycle Funnel™ is a better design and a necessary foundation to your funnel management success, it's just one component. Having just a BuyCycle Funnel™ is not sufficient to produce the kind of payoff you likely want. It's more than just about having a BuyCycle Funnel™. Let's see what that is.

Part Three:

It's Not Just About the Funnel

Chapter 5
It's About a Funnel *Process*

In chapter five of his second classic book, Good to Great, author Jim Collins compares two companies, Walgreens and Eckerd. Both companies grew for a long stretch of time during the 1980's and 1990's. Walgreens began pulling away from Eckerd in revenue in the 1980's and grew to twice the size in revenue as Eckerd by the early 1990's. Walgreens earned a billion dollars *more* in net profits than Eckerd did in that time period and Walgreens' cumulative stock returns for a two decade period ending in 2000 beat the stock market in general by a handsome margin. How did it do all of this? Collins says Walgreens committed to a hedgehog strategy, something he describes as simplifying the complexity of the world into a single organizing idea, a basic principle or concept that unifies and guides everything. For Walgreens, this single organizing idea was having the most convenient drugstores that achieve a high profit per customer visit. Everything Walgreens did regarding strategy and implementation centered on this concept. The company executed it with incredible consistency and discipline and the results speak for themselves.

Sales funnel management may seem to have little in common with running a drugstore chain. But there is at least one lesson for you funnel experts to draw from their story. While it was important for Walgreens to have a clever strategy of achieving high profit per customer visit, they followed through with a commitment to implementing and executing on that strategy. Let me be clear in translation: while the BuyCycle Funnel™ is a better model and is necessary to practicing effective funnel management, implementation and execution of a *funnel process* is key to funnel management success.

This begs the question then - what does a funnel process look like? I'll give you a peek at that right now because I think it will help you to have a picture of where I'm eventually taking you. However, we won't go into it with great detail yet. First, we've got to establish the mindset of needing process to manage the funnel function. Then we'll present fundamentals of a funnel management process, the building blocks if you will. The process will then make a lot more sense.

Breakthrough's 8-Step Process

Breakthrough's 8-Step Funnel Management Process is a proprietary and complete system for managing your sales funnel function.

The 8-Step Process begins where it should, by taking a competency assessment of your funnel management. You've got to know how good you funnel manage now to know if you're getting better at it later. The 8-Step Process links your sales objectives to the funnel. It also gives you a custom BuyCycle Funnel™ that is specific to your selling environment. It includes training and coaching to your funnel and to the process. It builds in regular inspections of the funnel called Funnel Audits and measures your progress toward qualitative and quantitative goals. Finally, we continue to assess your competency at prescribed future points to know how well you're doing overall and what needs to be improved.

In chapter ten, we go into greater detail of the 8-Step Process.

In this section, I'll make a case for committing to a funnel process by first making a case for having a process approach to your selling efforts overall. Think of this as answering the question 'why sales process?' Then we will give you the fundamental building blocks you'll need to build it. Finally, we'll cap it off with a chapter on coaching.

Sales Process: Heightened Awareness

Over the past several years there's been a lot of activity around the topic of sales process. Papers have been written about it. Books have been published about it. New sales training companies have been created because of it, and some existing companies have revamped and reorganized to provide process with their offerings.

As a result, many sales executives have become more aware of sales process. This is a good thing. Some have made attempts to implement it within their companies. Some of those have succeeded. Maybe you personally know of some that have not. Creating a sales process seems simple enough to understand but it's a hard thing to get right. It's a change initiative any way you look at it, and change can be painful. It takes a big commitment over time to make it work.

The national account manager of a client of mine expressed to me at the outset of our work with his company his satisfaction in the way we were going about helping his company create and implement a process for selling. He said, *"You're working back from where we want to be, and figuring out all the things we've got to do to get there. It all makes sense."* His is a healthy perspective to have and it's the right start to make their investment pay off. I have confidence that he and his colleagues will continue to make it work. Work is what it will take.

Creating a Culture of Sales Process

The emergence of sales process is an attempt to make sales more of a science than an art. To put greater predictability to the cause and effect of activities surrounding the sales function. Why? Well, look at how process has transformed other parts of business like operations and manufacturing and logistics and the supply chain. Through Six Sigma and lean manufacturing these business functions have improved. Sales has lagged these business functions in being run with discipline and structure. The sales artists and traditionalists might be put off by the whole process thing but the results show that a process investment for sales is a shift in the right direction.

> **"Process equals freedom."**

One of my clients who's a big fan of process is Bill O'Grady, Senior Vice President of US Distribution for Mass Mutual Retirement Services. Bill is a well known and respected sales leader in the financial services industry. I've had the good fortune of helping Bill improve the sales performance of a couple of his companies throughout his career by creating and implementing sales process for his teams. Bill believes so much in the power of process for selling he has a mantra he chants with his people: *"process equals freedom."* Bill understands that creating change in sales organizations requires vision, commitment and a relentless adherence to prescribed thought processes and business practices. His process equals freedom speech is given to his entire team each time we've rolled out the major initiative of building a sales process under his leadership.

At first, the phrase process equals freedom can seem to be a paradox, especially to those who haven't served under someone who leads this way. Process sounds restrictive and contained, while freedom suggests wide open and as you wish. But here's the hidden meaning. In a business world full of every day distractions and possibilities for how you spend your time, having a process for the way you sell eliminates many of those distractions and helps you focus on the right things. It also helps you continuously improve by helping you diagnose what you need to improve.

Process is a means to the end, an enabler to achieving sales goals. In <u>The New Solution Selling</u> by Keith Eades, he asks, *"Why have a process?"* He says it gives everyone a roadmap of what to do next and that leads to a higher probability of success. Amen to that. He also says that one of the five key elements of a sales process should include a management system that measures and reinforces and determines the probability of success. Think of process as giving you better data and better analysis, which leads to better decision making.

Process Is What Gets Managed

Another way of reinforcing what Eades says about process is to say that process is what gets managed. This may be obvious, but I assure you there will be times when you'll want to try to manage the outcome (results) instead of the path (process) to the outcome. But there are no shortcuts. If you play golf you can relate to it this way. You don't set out to shoot the round of your life as a golfer - you can't manage the final result, your score. You manage what you can control - your drives, your shot selection, your club choice, the number of greens you hit in regulation, your putting strategy (be aggressive or conservative), your management of risk, and of course your emotions. In many ways the result takes care of itself. The golfer who keeps track of all of her statistics like driving distance and accuracy, greens in regulation, putts per round, percentage of up and down, sand saves, one putts, and more knows what parts of her game need to be improved and then works on those.

The great Jack Nicklaus had a process for managing his game. First, to hit the best shot he'd consider the lie he had. That had a big influence on the type of shot he could hit. Then he considered variables such as the wind, temperature and even humidity. He considered the level of risk he was prepared to take on the shot. He decided what kind of shot he wanted to hit and then visualized hitting the shot by standing behind the ball and mentally hitting it. Then he approached the ball and set up in a very orderly, prescribed fashion and let it rip. This was his pre-shot routine and he never wavered from it. It was his process, and of course his results speak for themselves.

What's the Scope of Sales Process?

Recognize that process can be applied to many different areas of selling. Let's see where.

A Process for Strategic Account Management

You can have a sales process for a strategic account management function (and probably should if you get a fair share of business from these types of accounts). A process for this part of your business might include a funnel component, a strategic account criteria component, and some way to manage all of the resources that touch these types of customers. You might have a negotiation component. There's a lot at stake here. An excellent resource for strategic account management is the Strategic Account Management Association (called SAMA) based in Chicago.

Opportunity Management

You can put process to Opportunity Management, which is all about the demand generating side of your business – where and how and when you get new leads, qualify those leads, and win your fair share of them. If it sounds critical to your company's success, you're right. This part of selling includes things like target accounts, qualification criteria, a strategy piece, and even call planning and execution. Of course, opportunity management is a close cousin to funnel management.

Sales Call/Customer Facing Selling Methods

Since the one on one contact you have with customers and prospects is a moment of truth event, you'd expect that there's a lot of process that can be applied to making these interactions pay off.

Process applied to this part of selling puts structure to how you open the meeting, how you ask questions and learn about needs, how you share information that the customer needs to know, and how you ultimately wrap things up with an agreed upon next step.

Negotiation Strategy

If you've studied anything about the impact that effective negotiation can have on your bottom line and overall sales results, you won't be surprised to know that you can put process to negotiation. Like other parts of selling, negotiation has an underlying structure to it and can be approached systematically.

What's Not Process

One of the things that has had an impact on sales process is software such as CRM (customer relationship management) for managing account information, contacts, sales opportunities, customers and all of the history associated with them. This has been an interesting phenomena in the field of selling because the early data on performance of these investments isn't overwhelmingly impressive. While there are many specific reasons for this, one problem is the software should not be viewed as being the process. It automates the process.

> **Your software is not your process. Your software supports your process.**

A study in 2005 by a well known sales training company surveyed more than 3,000 executives and found that almost 80% of sales leaders surveyed were not convinced that CRM does a good job of defining an effective sales process for their companies. In another study of 1400 CRM installations by various companies in many different industries, 32% reported no improvement in performance and 37% reported only minor improvement. This is shocking when you consider the cost to implement CRM systems can routinely run a thousand or more dollars per person.

Part of the reason is due to companies not taking the time to define the problems they wanted these systems to solve. They got carried away with the capabilities of software and rushed to building solutions around it. If you start out by defining the problem you want to solve it sets you up for a successful outcome. Companies also didn't define and use their sales processes manually first, then apply CRM to automate the process.

Overall however, CRM software has had a positive effect. It's exposed the lack of structure for selling and measuring performance that many companies have which has prompted some of them to do something about it. It's also given sales leaders a visibility of the sales funnel for their entire business. Just having visibility itself doesn't magically provide great data – it's the old saying 'garbage in, garbage out'. Software doesn't ensure compliance to entering and updating funnel entries. What's needed is a reliable funnel management process that software supports. Without a funnel process that produces high integrity of data these funnels can easily mislead and do more harm than good.

Today More than Ever Process is Needed for Selling

Years ago, hard working salespeople could be lone rangers in selling, taking orders, even delivering product and troubleshooting after the sale. Today, sales is more about team work and collaborating and specialization. There is a different set of variables for the seller and his or her company to manage that usually requires a more collaborative approach to working with the customer and eventually getting things done.

Increased Competition

My clients universally tell me that there's more competition today. In many industries there are lower barriers to entry and new competitors coming in. Technology has made it possible for companies to rise quickly from a modest start. Sellers have to be decisive and quick to know how to strike and strategize to be successful. Sellers need to bring in their specialists to answer questions the prospect has. This increases the seller's credibility when he or she uses these resources.

Pricing Pressures

One of the ways new competitors get noticed is by offering their products and services at a discount to existing suppliers. It certainly gets the attention of customers. Since many of our clients sell premium priced solutions we are asked to help them use sales methods and techniques to defend their higher prices. Processes for selling and negotiating can be very effective at holding the line on prices and value propositions. Again, it goes back to what's getting managed. If there's no process to manage, then each salesperson is left up to his or her own abilities and knowledge to respond effectively. They might be tempted to discount to hit a month end quota or avoid losing a big sale. On the other hand, with process salespeople can better strategize and respond and perform.

Geographically Dispersed Selling Teams

Many companies have their salespeople and technical staff scattered all over the country or even the world. They come together through conference calls and by the internet to sell and work on customer issues. For example, my global tier one auto supplier has vehicle platforms it manages for customers through commercial and program management teams that have people in India, Germany, Korea, southeast Asia and North America. People from all of these regions often participate in global conference calls where sales strategy is discussed. It puts pressure on communicating clearly and timely and to be productive during these discussions.

A Culture of Cause and Effect

Although sales data – a lagging indicator – is still the primary gauge of how well a salesforce performs, sales leaders want to know with greater confidence the cause and effect of their salesforce's performance – real time. And sales data doesn't always give the truest picture. Just because Johnny closed a big deal doesn't mean Johnny's a great salesperson. Just because the entire salesforce is at 112% of plan for the year doesn't mean it is exhibiting effective sales behaviors. So what? If you don't know the cause and effect of your selling efforts you won't know what to keep doing well that you're doing well, and you won't know what you need to do different that you aren't doing so well. The head of sales can't afford to find out the hard way after the numbers post. The good news is that with process the head of sales can know earlier how well the team exhibits the right sales behaviors and what needs to happen to help the team improve and track to hit quota.

Process Gives You Good Data in a Timely Manner

One of the most common problems in sales organizations today is the lack of good data. Not the lagging indicator data like sales numbers but leading indicators like your funnel value, or what we called Total Viable Revenue back in Chapter 3. When you're staring at a quota GAP in July and a year end finish line that's getting closer every day you want an accurate answer to the question, *what is my funnel's ability right now to close enough business to achieve my quota?* Depending on the answer and a few other variables you might have time to act on this information to still achieve this year's quota. Total Viable Revenue as a leading indicator to sales is like what a heart rate monitor is to the runner during a race. If the monitor shows the runner working way too hard he might not be able to sustain that pace forever and his performance will suffer. The runner can slow down or try to relax to get the heart rate down and run a better race in the end.

Process produces good data that helps the sales leader accurately forecast. You already know that the BuyCycle Funnel™ produces better data than a traditional funnel. Having a process for rolling up the forecasts of each sales territory and each sales region to the overall business increases the accuracy of the forecast and lets all stakeholders in it act on that information. Even if the forecast will not be met it's less likely to be fatal if leaders know about it far enough in advance.

Process Should Simplify

Having a process for selling simplifies. As a salesperson you are bombarded with things to do and think about and act on every day, both from customers and from the home office. The best thing a salesperson can do to remain productive is to focus on the things that really matter. Remember O'Gradys 'process equals freedom' mantra. Here's one simple example. If you respect the need to commit to ongoing prospecting to find new leads then why not block out a day or half a day a week or every other week to that function? Go to your calendar and block it out right now. You might say that's not reasonable because you might have to respond to unpredictable customer requests or home office demands. I understand that things come up. But if something you highly value isn't committed to on your calendar routinely, I think your actions speak louder than your words. As for prospecting for new business, you'll pay the price sooner or later if you continue to let it take a back seat to other important things.

Process serves as a simplifier because it helps you say no to things that are not part of your process. For example, if you get a lead that is obviously not in your sweet spot for selling, your process should immediately flag it and help you decide how you're going to respond to the lead.

Process Helps Teams Communicate

Improved communication is probably one of the biggest benefits of having a sales process. When there's one defined process that all salespeople work within, communication is faster and better. One defined sales process helps sales work better with other departments such as marketing, sales support, engineering and others. On the other hand when there are 50 different ways to get something done, even if some of them are effective, it's chaotic. It's a productivity killer that costs you money.

The head of a strategic account sales team for one of my clients told me that a sales funnel process we designed for him cut by fifty percent the amount of time he spent on his weekly funnel conversations with salespeople. Before, he was spending way too much time simply interpreting what each sales person meant regarding funnel topics and items.

Process Helps Sales Managers Coach and Develop

One of the greatest benefits of sales processes is in how they have improved the quality of coaching. Much of this is due to clearer communication between manager and salesperson. Managers are often former successful salespeople who have a strong notion of how salespeople should sell. But if the manager is younger or has fewer years of selling than his people who are older and with more years of selling, the manager can struggle to get credibility with this audience. The veteran thinks *"what can this young manager tell me about selling?"*, and the manager thinks *"I can't get through to this salesperson because he doesn't give me credibility."* However, with sales process that both the veteran and the sales manager have been trained in the manager can explain and even defend his or her comments and position by referring to the process. The comments are no longer just what the manager thinks. They are what good processes lead them to understand. It opens the eyes of the veteran salespeople who might otherwise resist the coaching.

Process Helps Sales Managers Transfer Knowledge

Another challenge facing some sales managers is the opposite of the younger manager / veteran salesperson situation. It's when the sales manager is recognized as having lots of experience but struggles to pass that experience on to his or her salespeople.

Let's say a manager makes a sales call with one of her salespeople. During the call she sees him making a mistake or two but nothing that is fatal to the call objective. When they finish and get back to the car she has a brief post-call discussion, always a good idea when traveling with your salespeople. But instead of saying here's how I would have done it, she walks him through their process for making sales calls. She leads him through the opening, the questioning, and the seeking of commitment. She asks him to remember what he said and how he said it. She refers to the process throughout the conversation and gets him to see how he performed against it. The coaching therefore is not about the sales manager's style or approach; it's about compliance to their sales call planning and execution process.

Process Helps You Manage Proactively

Finally, process will help you get through one of the biggest challenges salespeople face today – being more proactive and less reactive. Companies have put more and more duties and tasks on the backs of their salespeople often due to cutbacks in staff. They rely even more on technology to save time. Some companies expect their salespeople to be on call 24/7. As a result it puts pressure on salespeople to shortcut the sales cycle and win business faster. They're tempted to see low hanging fruit as the answer regardless of how poor a fit some of these opportunities are to the company's target criteria. It causes them to think less strategically which reduces the number of better qualified opportunities, which means they've got to rely more on the low hanging fruit, and so on. It almost becomes a cycle.

What process does probably more than anything else is it helps you say no to things that are tempting but not effective. For example, if you decide that selling to companies that have no loyalty to their suppliers is not a good use of your time and resources, then process helps you say no to those opportunities when they knock on your door. What do you do with that time now? You go find opportunities to sell to companies that have a track record and culture of rewarding loyalty.

Also, let's say you know you've got to spend 6 hours a week prospecting for new leads and you carve out every Tuesday to do that. What do you do if a client says I need you to come by next Tuesday to check something out for us? No, you don't say I'm prospecting and can't make it. But if you make a habit of immediately saying *sure I'll be there* instead of asking *would Wednesday work? I'm already committed to something important on Tuesday*, then you're allowing yourself to be held captive by the client – and you show little respect for your process for lead generation. It might sound easier to say than to do, but no one said process was going to be easy.

A client of mine responded this way to the topic of committing to process to be more effective. He complained about not having enough time in a day to get things done. He was incredibly busy but he didn't feel that he was effective. I told him he needed to step back and identify his top priorities, the things that would have real impact on his position. He should first make time for these important things then get to the rest of his tasks. He replied that putting that kind of structure to his schedule would be too restrictive – *"how will I possibly get everything done?"* he commented. You don't get everything done and that's ok and that's the point.

The Prevalence of Sales Process Today

With all of these benefits you'd think that companies would easily justify the time and effort needed to create sales processes and get right to it. However, salespeople can be a stubborn lot. We're fiercely independent, we're driven and we can have strong opinions about things. Also, since process has been fairly recent to sales many of the sales leaders who would lead an investment in process weren't raised in that kind of an environment, so they don't know how to approach it. But I keep seeing process becoming more common and that's a good thing.

In a paper published by the Harvard Business Review, the authors cite several sample cases of companies that have put process to their selling efforts and have much to show in payoff for the investment. My favorite is one that shows how a division of General Electric put process to targeting accounts, determining where it should focus its selling efforts to attract new business. The results of the segmenting showed that the top thirty percent of prospective customers were three times more likely to do a deal with General Electric than the bottom seventy percent. Holy cow! What's more, barely half of these top thirty percent of prospects had been *previously* labeled as a high priority by the manager, probably getting little prospecting attention by the salespeople.

From Sales Process to Sales Funnel Process

If process for sales makes so much sense and funnel management is a subset of sales, then logic says process for funnel management must also make sense. Again, in the spirit of becoming a student of your craft, the more you understand why process makes so much sense for managing the funnel the better you'll be at this crucial business function.

It may seem that managing the funnel is a contained issue – one that is largely within the sales person's responsibility and maybe the sales manager. It's not. How well the funnel is managed affects not only the sales person and manager but the entire business. For example, think of forecasting. If one sales person in a company with 100 sales people reports a $100,000 deal is highly likely to close, but in reality it's not, that may have limited adverse affect on the VP of sales. But if the other 99 sales people in that salesforce are doing the same thing - each one reporting a $100,000 deal as being highly likely to close, when they shouldn't be labeled that way - now that VP has a $10M problem. One of my clients with over 100 sales people agreed with this, with one exception. Their deal sizes are more like half a million dollars. So that VP of sales has a $50M problem to deal with.

> **A sustainable, positive change in the company's funnel performance comes best when the company commits to a funnel process for the business.**

Because managing the sales funnel is not just a salesperson issue, the solution should not be seen as a salesperson issue. Rather, a sustainable, positive change in the company's funnel performance comes best from the company committing to a funnel process *for the business*. This is a top down initiative committed to from the bottom up. The company president must sponsor it and get others to buy in because other departments are affected. Marketing, manufacturing, service, finance all depend on funnel data. If the funnel is managed poorly and it contains bad data, then it's harder to make good business decisions. The president's sponsorship shows his or her commitment even if the architect of the process is the head of sales. Someone has to drive it and sales should.

An Interdependency of Sales Funnel Data

The interdependency of funnel data is at two levels. One is within the realm of sales, that chain from the sales person up to the head of sales. The other level involves the non-sales functions such as manufacturing, production, marketing, and finance and any others that also rely on the business having good funnel data. Let's look at both of these.

Interdependency Within Sales

Funnel data helps the sales person manage her territory. She needs to know at any time during the year her funnel's ability to close the additional business needed to hit quota. For the same reason, funnel data helps the sales manager manage his or her district or region – all of the funnels of the sales people under his or her responsibility. After all, the manager has a quota to achieve too.

With forecasting being a primary responsibility of the VP of Sales this person is relying on the sales managers to produce good funnel data and accurate forecasts themselves. The VP needs to know if forecast will be achieved – and early enough to take corrective action or to avoid surprises. The problem is that without a funnel process, many VPs rely on gut feel and intuition to accomplish the task.

The process commonly goes like this. The VP asks the managers what business is going to close in their regions for the period. The managers go to their sales people and ask them the same question. The managers do this for all sales people, then add the total, and report a forecast number up to the VP. The smart people know that their credibility is on the line when they claim that certain business will close in the period, so they're tempted to sandbag a bit. The rookies want to show their managers how hard they're working and tend to overstate what business will close. The smart manager knows this about each of his or her people and makes subjective judgments for each one. Then she considers her boss's needs before settling on a final forecast number that she delivers. I know some managers who are quite good at doing this. But they rely on an incredible knowledge of their marketplace and of their people.

With all due respect to these pros this is a way for the manager or sales person to be successful, but not a way for the business to be successful. Some might say this forecasting by feel is simply the way it's done and managers must learn to get good at it or else. It tends to be the way it's done, but I disagree that the answer is to just get better at forecasting this way. What happens when the region has turnover and the manager must learn the forecasting nuances of the new sales people? There's a learning curve the manager must go through – does this rep tend to sandbag, or overstate her funnel? Another problem with this is that when salespeople have all the information about their funnels they sometimes will reveal only what's required to management or will spin the information to first serve their needs. This may sound like a criticism of the salesperson, but it's really a criticism of management not putting better processes in place.

The Solution Must be Lead by Sales

Overcoming this hurdle of lack of process should get CEO or President sponsorship, but then sales must lead the charge for putting a system in place. Unfortunately, I meet sales managers every day who tell me they know this funnel stuff is important, but believe that selling and sales funnel management is about hiring the right people and having an account list within a software program and that's it. They believe they can 'talent their way through this', hire veterans who 'get it' and the job is taken care of. Interdependency of funnel data demands more than just talent. Funnel management is no more about veterans who get it than achieving record levels of product quality on a production line is about the line workers working harder. You need good people *and* you need good processes.

Interdependency With Non-Sales Functions

Since the impact of the sales funnel reaches beyond sales to other parts of the business, it gives us even more reason to build a better process for the entire function.

The Funnel for Marketing

Funnel data is valuable to marketing. Since the funnel is an indicator of the customer's buying process, marketing can contribute more to the sales efforts with targeted collateral and campaigns. Funnel data lets marketing more effectively plan and forecast for product lines. It helps marketing track the success of new product launches. We've found that some of our clients have used the BuyCycle Funnel™ to bring marketing and sales closer together. It defines an overall sales process that helps both departments collaborate more effectively.

A funnel system is valuable for product managers. They likely have a budget or number to achieve for the year for their products just like a salesperson or sales manager has a number to achieve for the sales territory or region. Everything around that product manager's line is dependent on bringing in the necessary sales to support the line. One of my clients, a young marketing manager, said the BuyCycle Funnel™ approach sounded great for the new product she was about to introduce to the marketplace. She was on the hook for this product to achieve about a specific revenue number in the first year. The only indicator she would have of being on track throughout the year was sales tracings from the distributor – a lagging indicator. Even worse, this lagging indicator was about 60 days after the sales were made. So, sales that closed at the end of June wouldn't show up on the tracings until the first of September. If the numbers weren't at plan for the year she'd have only four months left in the year to change course. Most sales organizations aren't that nimble. Salespeople are not likely to dramatically shift sales focus from existing bread and butter products and top accounts to selling a new product that barely makes a blip to their compensation. With a funnel process the product manager can proactively respond to funnel data that tells her the health of her product funnel and the likelihood of achieving her numbers.

The Funnel for Production and Manufacturing

Funnel data is also valuable for production and manufacturing, who rely on expected sales to determine how much to build or buy. The president of one of my clients reinforced this to me. He told us the better his salespeople could predict what was coming, the better his company would know how much to build. This means it could prevent having out of stock situations or back orders or the other problem of having too much inventory.

The Funnel for Finance and the CEO

As the executives who are most responsible for the financial health and results of the business, the CFO and CEO need funnel data to carry out their responsibilities. Funnel data is valuable for forecasting and forecasting accurately is necessary to make good business decisions. The CEO is accountable to shareholders or private investors to deliver an acceptable return and to lead the company toward a successful future. Consider this actual global press release for a client of mine:

While (the company) started the year with improved backlogs, they are still not at levels necessary for adequate profitability, although the pipeline of prospective new business is high.

The company is telling its shareholders about its business condition today and how that condition will affect the business going forward – and is doing so by describing the state of its sales funnel. What do you think the conversation between the president of this company and the board is like at the time of the press release? My guess is it's a short one - *"Well Carla, what's the number you're predicting for the end of this coming quarter?"* And what if results for the previous quarter were an unpleasant surprise – then it's a two question conversation: *"Carla, what happened?"* And what are you doing to prevent that from happening again?" With a business process for managing the company's funnel the president can have a more accurate reply to the first question and can avoid unpleasant surprises like the second one.

Contrast this interdependency with the alternative. Each department can do its own thing and occasionally come together to talk. Sales will tell marketing to leave them alone and let them sell. Marketing will create strategy and positioning without input from sales. Product development will design and build things they think are useful, without talking to marketing and customers first. This may sound like business practice from the ice ages – until you consider that it's still done this way in some companies.

I've probably said enough about the value of process for selling. Let's get into creating and adopting a BuyCycle Funnel™ Management process.

Chapter 6

Creating and Adopting a BuyCycle Funnel™ Process

In the last chapter we made a case for putting process to your sales function. I hope you are beginning to believe that the investment is worth the effort. In this chapter we'll lay out the fundamental building blocks to creating a process specifically for your sales funnel management function.

Let me say it this way: If you're a golfer and you want to seriously improve your game you need to hit better golf shots or hit good shots more consistently. But you don't do that by working directly on your *swing* - you work on the fundamentals that make up the swing. These fundamentals include the grip, grip pressure, the alignment, position of hands, ball position, weight distribution at set up, weight transfer during the swing, the take away, swing plane, pace, tension in your swing, and more. The outcome of your swing – the shot you hit - is greatly affected by all of these variables. To improve the outcome you need to improve these fundamentals.

It's the same for managing your sales funnel. It's not just about the funnel as I stated at the beginning of this section. To hit quota year after year, or get more salespeople in your salesforce hitting quota, you'll need to master the fundamentals that make up the *funnel process*.

Since I have no way to know which role you play in your company, that is, salesperson, sales manager, head of sales, head of marketing, head of the entire business, or some other role I'll write this chapter as if I've been asked to address an audience that might include all of you and to speak on the topic of fundamentals of building a sales funnel management process. While the salesperson is concerned with hitting quota, the sales manager wants that too, but also might have a forecasting responsibility to the VP of Sales. The manager also is responsible for developing salespeople. The VP of Sales definitely has a forecasting responsibility to someone senior to him or her, and needs to hit quota or plan. The VP also spends money on capital projects and human development and needs to know with high accuracy the kind of year the business is likely to have. If you're the CEO or President you'll want reliable forecasts from your VP of Sales to help you manage at the highest level, and to convey to shareholders and investors the state of the business.

Creating a Vision

One of the best places to start to create a funnel management process is with your vision. An executive at one of my largest clients validated this to me during one of our early sales meetings. She said *"I want to create the world's best sales organization."* Wow! That's the beginning of a vision. It might need a lot of work and specificity but it paints a strong visual for anyone who hears it.

Having a vision for the sales organization says we're more than just about our products and services. And in a world of shorter product life cycles, technology advancements, and global networks you'd better have more than just good products or services to sell. A vision helps define the way you're going to do business. If you're a Malcolm Baldridge quality award winning company or are trying to be one you're going to invest in process and people and continuous improvement. A vision helps define training and other needs. My client that wants to create the world's best sales organization had better be prepared to make investments in people, process, talent recruitment and retention, and ways to measure the impact all of this stuff has on the business. It's not a small undertaking. But it might give her the competitive edge her business needs.

> **A vision of having a world class funnel competency suggests best of the best, well managed, organized, disciplined, high achieving and more.**

Shift to vision for funnel management: A vision of creating a 'world class funnel competency', something we introduced in a previous chapter, is a statement of what you want your salesforce to be competent in. A vision of having a world class funnel competency suggests best of the best, well managed, organized, disciplined, high achieving and more. If you sell your team on the idea that this competency is the best path to achieving sales objectives consistently, then they'll be more likely to get on board your vision and commit with you to the destination.

With the vision as your picture of what you want to be, you can more easily define the tangible objectives that are needed to accomplish it. These objectives get tied to everything you do with your salesforce – the processes you give it to achieve the objectives, the recruiting and retention efforts you make to attract and keep the right people, the measurement of their productivity, and so on. You link your sales process to those goals and have a connected path from daily activity by the salesperson to the goals and vision you've defined. It's more likely to get the team to adoption of your funnel process and lasting changes in sales behavior.

I don't want to be critical of anyone who's not prepared to make the commitments necessary to adopt a sales process. It's a big undertaking. Some company cultures will absolutely not support this kind of approach and it will never work. For others, it'll be tempting to take short cuts.

Define Sales Goals and Objectives

While many sales organizations don't have a vision, most have their sales goals defined.   These goals are mainly defined by revenue and market share and sales productivity or sales efficiency (such as increasing close rate).   What's missing however in a lot of sales process efforts is a link between the process and the sales goals. *The BuyCycle Funnel is this link.*

For example, let's say your company is introducing a new product and you're the product manager or head of marketing. You likely have a quota for that product, even if it's not huge. You'll want the salesforce to spend sufficient mind share selling the product because it won't jump out of the bag and off the shelf all by itself. Doesn't it make sense to 'funnel' this new product to know at any time during the year the likelihood of hitting plan? And to be able to change selling strategies quickly enough if the funnel's ability to hit plan is not tracking well? With a BuyCycle Funnel™ process you can.

Or, let's say your business is rocking. You have more leads than you can handle. If you're not careful your salesforce might close more business than your capacity can handle, and they'll over promise and under deliver. You'll go from having high stock with your customers to losing credibility with them and possibly future sales. I've had sales leaders tell their salespeople to slow it down when their funnels look like this.

Using a funnel process, you'll know about this situation before it happens. You'll be able to rein in the selling efforts or maybe you can expand capacity. It might be just the rationale you need to sell your CEO and head of manufacturing on investing in greater capacity.

Finally, let's say you have sixty percent of your business tied up with four customers. You're feeling nervous about this and wish to spread the risk over a slightly larger customer base. With a funnel process you can target new customers that meet your profile, invest selling time in them and diversify your customer base.

Define Terms of Use

Implementing a funnel management process will likely mean doing things different. It's change. The more you define the terms of use of the process the easier people will understand your expectations of how it's to be used. Two ways to do this are with <u>reporting</u> and <u>dialogue</u>.

Reporting

Although reports can be viewed as a nuisance to salespeople, good reports provide valuable data to analyze and run the business. Most sales reports have limited use for funnel management because they are lagging indicators. The data is about past events, sales, and you can't do anything about something that has passed. What you need to run your business is a leading indicator report using the BuyCycle Funnel™. One report that we give clients is a BuyCycle Dashboard. It's a snapshot of important funnel data such as quota GAP, Total Viable Revenue and Funnel Factor. It tells the salesperson and manager quickly the funnel's ability to achieve the quota. Another report we provide is one that shows more data on the sales opportunities behind the Dashboard. It supplements what the Dashboard gives. If you have reports already through your software it's not hard to replace them with BuyCycle Funnel™ reports.

One of my clients created a funnel report that is part of its business plan review that its sales managers hold monthly with their salespeople. They use an excel spreadsheet format that is easy to understand. This review isn't a three hour drill down – it's an hour long for most managers. The report gives the right kind of opportunity information and a lot of it, aggregate to the funnel to let the managers have productive dialogue with their people.

Dialogue

If there's one thing my clients constantly remind me of it is that the BuyCycle Funnel™ is about having the right dialogue around sales opportunities. By committing scheduled time to discussing opportunities and your funnel you'll improve your funnel competency faster.

What does this look like? One of my clients has a top opportunity discussion by conference call every Friday with his region salespeople. Each salesperson gets 10-15 minutes to discuss the top 2-3 top opportunities he or she is working. They quickly use the BuyCycle Funnel™ to confirm where the opportunities are in the customer's buying process and then shift to creating sales strategies to advance the sale.

What's even better than scheduled conversations like this is to have BuyCycle Funnel™ dialogue on the spot or on an as needed basis. When this happens, it's a good sign that the adoption is taking place.

Create a Custom BuyCycle Funnel™

As I've explained earlier, you'll want to have a BuyCycle Funnel™ that's custom designed for your selling environment.

> **A custom BuyCycle Funnel™ defined by your customer's buying process is the most accurate description of what's happening in your selling environment.**

Having a BuyCycle Funnel™ specific to your selling environment is beneficial for several reasons. One, when the stages are defined by your customer's buying process the BuyCycle Funnel™ is the most accurate description of what's actually happening in your selling environment. Two, a custom funnel gives the system greater credibility in your organization and is more likely to be used. Three, the process of defining your own BuyCycle Funnel™ is incredibly valuable. You learn things about your selling approach and your environment including assumptions you're making about these things. Plus, by involving in the BuyCycle Funnel design stakeholders from non-sales departments like marketing or service or engineering you help them understand the sales function better.

Have a Physical Place for Your Funnel

To manage the funnel you've got to have it in a physical place. Each territory or salesperson has to enter the opportunity information somewhere and be able to see the funnel in total with a simple report. This can be as simple as an excel spreadsheet or much more sophisticated like a CRM (customer relationship management) system. If you have a contact manager program for accounts and contacts it might have a feature for creating new opportunities and organizing them in a basic way. You simply list each opportunity and create basic columns such as the dollar value of the opportunity, the account name, the products/services being considered, the close date, and the funnel stage. Sometimes clients will add a column for 'next action client' which I like because it puts the focus on what the customer needs to do next for the opportunity to advance.

Commit to Regular Inspection

One of the most important fundamentals of effective funnel management is to commit to regular inspection of your funnel. With the 8-Step Process we call these Funnel Audits.

> **A Funnel Audit is a structured conversation about your funnel that answers the question "what is my funnel's ability right now to close enough business to achieve quota?"**

A Funnel Audit is a structured analysis of your funnel. It's not complicated and it shouldn't take more than an hour or so. When the manager does Funnel Audits with salespeople it's like having a conversation, albeit one with a specific flow and format. It helps answer that most important question the salesperson should be asking throughout the year, *"What is your funnel's ability right now to close enough business to achieve your quota for the year?"*

The answer to the question directs you to how to spend your time over the next 30-60 days, which is the real payoff of good funnel management. If your funnel's ability is awesome you still set a plan of action to manage it. If your funnel's ability is poor, you set a plan of action to correct that. Because the funnel is changing all of the time as you find new leads, pursue some and not pursue others, win some sales, and lose some sales, your funnel's ability to hit your quota is likely also changing all of the time. The only way to stay on top of these changes and how they are affecting your ability to achieve quota is by inspecting the funnel regularly. Funnel Audits are best done between manager and salesperson to give the salesperson another perspective and to challenge him or her to ask the tough questions.

The term Funnel Audit might suggest something negative, similar to what happens to some people and their taxes. But it's precisely what is needed. This funnel stuff is serious business because achieving quota is serious business, both for the company and for the individual. Salespeople need to set aside any reservations about feeling put on the spot and being defensive. The pros don't mind.

Many of my clients comment that doing Funnel Audits gives them a constant defense against operating in a reactive state. It's common that salespeople do more than just sell; they're putting out fires, they're following up on issues, even tracking down payments. They're doing administrative stuff. It's easy to get sucked into things that have very little to do with selling – and be mislead into thinking that a full week of work was also a productive one from a selling perspective. It's easily possible that a salesperson works a 60 hour week and spends less than a tenth of that time actually selling. Funnel Audits put a stake in the ground for the need to commit time to selling and being productive in how you do it.

Define Your Quota and Funnel Period

This may seem obvious, but let's review a couple of important details of Funnel Audits and the rest of the 8-Step Process.

Much of the premise behind achieving a world class funnel competency is that you have a quota you're trying to achieve. The 8-Step Process helps you know how you're doing at any time at achieving it by giving you leading indicator information that you can act on. Without a quota, a funnel system is not directed at a concretely defined revenue target. In a way, it's like being a golfer and wanting to get better but never keeping score to know, measurably, if you really are getting better. Sure there are qualitative measures to sales (and to golf too) and the BuyCycle Funnel™ still gives you useful information about selling activity around the funnel. But without a quota there's likely no consequence if a quota is not achieved. The value of the funnel system with these kinds of environments is limited to using the BuyCycle Funnel™ as your opportunity management guide – which is still valuable. Remember, managing the lead from discovery to close is one of the two main functions of a funnel.

Most of the time the funnel period is for the company's fiscal year. It's likely that you'll be carrying two funnels at some time during one year, one for the year you're actively selling in and another one for the next year. You might be finding and qualifying new sales opportunities for next year's funnel as early as late summer or fall of the current year. For companies that have a very long sales cycle such as 18 months or longer you've got to be constantly managing more than one funnel. One of my clients manages funnels three years out. Remember the client who in August of 2007 was already at 125% to plan for 2008? His cycle was 18-24 months out and he was consciously working future funnels.

Measure the Effectiveness

The process wouldn't be complete if it didn't include measurement.

Breakthrough's 8-Step Process includes measurement. We start with benchmarks of your funnel competency. We know exactly where and why you're strong and weak with funnel management. We measure your progress after implementing the first few steps of the process. You'll know how well your funnel management efforts are paying off and what areas need attention.

Summary

These fundamentals might seem simple and straightforward. We've learned them through the years through trial and error. While they are simple they're not always easy to put into practice. You know that change can be tough. But for executives committed to producing lasting and significant improvement in sales performance the 8-Step Process for Funnel Management is a surefire way to achieve that.

Chapter 7

Coaching: The Heart of the 8-Step Process

Sales managers, this chapter's for you.

A client was in my home office recently for a coaching session and did something that reinforced how important it is to ask the right questions when coaching and developing people.

We were in my office when my two daughters came home from school. Polly is twelve and in the seventh grade and Hannah is fourteen and in the eighth grade. I called down and told them to come up to meet someone. I take the opportunity when I can to have them introduce themselves to others, especially adults, to help them get comfortable meeting new people and presenting themselves appropriately. You know, using a firm handshake, looking people in the eyes and saying their names.

They came up to the office and I said "Girls, please meet Mr. Bridgewater." One at a time they extended their hands, looked Pete in the eye, said their names and said it is nice to meet you. Then he asked the most popular question that all school kids get asked by parents when they come home from school. *"How was school today?"* You know the answer: *"Good."* And with that one question he shut them down and killed the dialogue.

Pete knew better. For one, he has kids of his own. He knows that if he wants to really know what happened at school that's the one question he should avoid. We joked about it afterward because our session that day was all about how to build Pete's coaching competency with his people, a competency that is facilitated by asking BuyCycle Funnel™ *process-based* questions to promote the right kind of dialogue between Pete and his salespeople. It's key to getting them to adopt the BuyCycle Funnel™ as a way of thinking and executing. You build your coaching through that questioning. The process leads you to asking the right kinds of questions. You lead, not spoon feed. Your people learn faster and better. You make an impact.

In this chapter written for the sales manager we'll see how BuyCycle Funnel™ Management gives you a new and effective focus to getting the right dialogue to happen between you and your salespeople. You'll see how asking the right questions promotes this dialogue. You'll see that your role as a coach to your salespeople is shaped by four underlying principles that guide your coaching output and set you up for successful coaching. Things done in your own style, but within a solid framework that your people understand.

The BuyCycle Funnel™ is a New Muscle Memory

Adopting the BuyCycle Funnel™ is hard because it's change. The challenge is in getting people to change the way they think about their funnels and sales opportunities and to *replace* some existing way they think about these things with a BuyCycle Funnel™ way of thinking and executing. That's your challenge in your role as coach. You want to get your people to adopt the new way and make it second nature or a new 'muscle memory', a term that golfers use to describe their swings and getting in the zone. Golfers want to get beyond having to think about how to swing and let the muscle memory take over so they can <u>execute</u> their way around the golf course effectively. Same thing we're shooting for with the BuyCycle Funnel™ and the 8-Step Process. Let me suggest four coaching principles or what I call The Coaching Mindset that can guide you as you play the role of coach.

Coaching Mindset

Principle One – Coaches are leaders.

Whether it's learned or it comes naturally, leadership plays a big part in the style and context of the effective sales coach. First off, the good sales managers see themselves as leaders. They know that their mission is to extract every ounce of energy from their people toward the outcome of selling more, and they realize that each person might require a unique approach. They are people that their salespeople want to work for and are motivated to work for. Bill Holehouse, VP of Sales for Cott Systems, knows this well. In 2006 he challenged his people to hit a sales number by the end of the year by telling them he'd shave his head if they reached it. They did. But he didn't just stop by the barbershop and show up bald – he sat on a chair in the middle of his office and his salespeople took turns with the razor. It was quite a picture.

Principle Two - Coaches promote discovery.

An effective coach challenges his people to learn and discover. Throughout the sale and especially at the beginning. With all of the people typically involved in a buying process, with competing motivations and different degrees of urgency and complacency, and all of the other variables surrounding the buying process there's a tremendous amount of complexity at work. To be an effective coach you've got to get your people to cut through that to get to the core of not just problems but intentions by certain people in the account to resolve those problems.

Many of my clients are engineers who are now selling. They have a natural curiosity and problem solving mentality about them. I tell them that they need to shift their curiosity to understanding the customer's buying process if they want to be more successful in sales. With a sales process to channel that curiosity they can be very effective at playing the sales role.

Principle Three - Coaches challenge assumptions.

Good sales managers challenge the assumptions their salespeople make. And process helps them do that. One place in particular where this has high impact is with sales veterans. They're often a challenge for the sales manager because these veterans can believe they're the only ones who really know what's going on in their territories and in their accounts. The process is how you speak to them and how you organize your thoughts. A process does help you understand the customer and the territory quicker and therefore gives you more credibility with the sales veteran who might not be open to your suggestions.

With a process you can walk them down the path of how their customers buy. The process isn't something *you've* thought up; it's what's been validated by others as being true. You use the process to challenge the assumptions your salespeople make about the people, their motivations or lack of, and their intent to really commit to resolving the problems they've shared with you.

Principle Four - Coaches facilitate execution.

Good sales coaches help their salespeople execute well. Executing well has a big impact in being consistently successful in sales. Process is your tool.

Execution simply means making sure you effectively complete the tasks that make up your process. You want to execute on good sales calls and good strategy for sales opportunities. You want to execute on the action plans your funnel analysis leads you to. What good is the analysis otherwise?

Facilitating execution means removing barriers to getting things done. It means not letting things get complicated. Keep your salespeople focused on the fundamentals and do them well. For funnel management, you're on your way to having a new framework for executing effectively on the most important function of your job.

A Framework is Necessary

Throughout the book I've talked about frameworks and processes because I want you to see that achieving breakthroughs in your sales performance through effective funnel management is much more than remembering tips and techniques. Having a framework to coach your salespeople through it, the 8-Step Process, will help you be more consistent, more productive, and more valuable.

In the book <u>Good to Great</u>, author Jim Collins writes that great companies have a culture of *discipline*. They have defined ways of thinking about things and doing things – they have frameworks. These frameworks are the ways of thinking and behaving that their people coach to and lead by. Great companies don't just have good and hard working people with good intentions running around being busy. They use processes and frameworks to channel those assets.

For the sales manager, having the framework of the BuyCycle Funnel™ and the 8-Step Funnel Management Process helps you do something to have one of your biggest impacts with your people - have productive conversations with them with the right dialogue.

The Right Dialogue and the Things That Really Matter

A framework like the BuyCycle Funnel™ promotes the right dialogue simply because it comes with a set of terms and phrases that is meant to facilitate communication. When everyone on the team has been trained and coached in these terms and phrases it's easier to communicate. For example, we've defined a Viable Opportunity as one where the person of authority to spend the money says it's ok to do that. A Viable Opportunity is also part of the funnel value we call Total Viable Revenue. Though it takes a little time to adopt these terms, once you do they help you and your salespeople cut through lots of noise to get to the things that really matter.

If you ever discount the value of something like this that promotes the right dialogue, just remember Pete's conversation with my kids. It happens every day when kids come home from school and their parents ask them that dialogue killer, "how was school today?" And if you're busy like my wife and I are, and you're trying to stay connected to their world, then you want to avoid these kinds of questions. Conversations like this also happen every day between sales managers and their salespeople and if they aren't structured by a framework they can be just as useless.

The sales manager equivalent of the *'how was school today?'* question is something like *'how did the call go with so and so this week?'* What's the common response? *"Good."* And as a manager you haven't learned a thing. You've removed your chance of making a difference with this salesperson in that moment. And while one moment isn't such a big deal, the hundreds or even thousands of them that you have each year with your people are – the result is they get robbed of development. They don't grow and improve. And that's a big role you play with them.

Sometimes the question is centered on the <u>sales opportunity</u> and what's been happening with it. It goes something like this:

Manager: So how's it going with Trident Enterprises?

Salesperson: Oh, pretty good.

Manager: So how's it looking?

Salesperson: It looks pretty good. I've got a good relationship with the director of purchasing. I think our chances are close to 80% on this one.

Manager: Sounds good. Keep me posted.

You laugh at this, but if you're a manager and had a tape recorder of some of your own conversations with your people…

The right dialogue is important because it surfaces what's important in the sale and for sales calls. You can then help the salesperson make intelligent decisions on that information. It goes back to two of the four principles we presented earlier, promote discovery and challenge assumptions. If you're not doing this with your people then your impact has to be in question. For example, when one of your salespeople makes an important sales call what do you really want to surface about the call? Things like this:

- Does the customer perceive a problem? What it is?

- What did you learn about it?

- What didn't you learn about it that might be important?

- How does he or she see it affecting her personally?

- How much and what kind of influence does she have to do something about this problem?

- Who else does it affect and how?

- Who doesn't care that much about this problem but still has influence on whether or not something gets done about it?

- Did you find out if this person is committed to doing something about those problems?

- Will this person introduce you to other people that you need to see in the sale?

- Is this person the one authorized to spend money to fix this problem? If not, then who is and can this person make an introduction for you?

- Did anyone commit to doing anything right now about this situation?

The answers to these questions are necessary for good selling. This is the kind of information that constitutes the right dialogue and it's the information that the BuyCycle Funnel™ gives you. It makes it possible for you to consistently have good conversations with your salespeople, but you'll need to commit to a few things to make it pay off.

1. **You'll need to become the expert in the process.** This should come as no surprise. If you're expecting your people to use the BuyCycle Funnel™ they'll expect you to use it yourself.

2. **You need to show your people that you're committed to making the process a way of running the business.** You can't do this half way. They'll see right through it. It's human nature for your people to resist a change in the way they sell and they might take every chance they get to challenge your commitment to this new way. If you give in, you're a goner, and your credibility will take a hit.

3. **You'll need to make time for BuyCycle dialogue.** This seems simple enough. It's like the saying that showing up is half the challenge. But you know that your time is in constant demand and it's tempting to hit the surface with your coaching and not allocate good time to sales conversations with your people. Don't think that the process will take a lot of time. What's likely is that you'll simply replace current dialogue with BuyCycle dialogue, so it's time you're already spending on sales discussions. In some cases you might even spend less time because the conversations are more productive.

Coaching Your Sales Team – One Person at a Time

One of the common responses we get about the BuyCycle Funnel™ is that it easily adapts to veteran salespeople as well as to those with less sales tenure. If your sales team has a mix of both levels of tenure the model will serve you well.

The reason for the model's adaptability is simple – it's based on the customer's buying cycle. While we get few arguments that that's where the selling focus should be, we see all too often all levels of salespeople not selling this way. You'd think that veteran salespeople would be better at selling to the customer's buying process, but they are just as guilty of making assumptions during the sale as the rookies are. Let's first see how you can use the BuyCycle Funnel™ and the 8-Step Process to coach these veterans, and then see how you can use it to coach others.

Coaching the Sales Veteran

To coach a veteran in BuyCycle Funnel™ selling, you've got to think like a veteran.

First off, veteran salespeople have more years of developing habits than those with less tenure. Good habits and bad habits. In fifteen, twenty or more years of selling they've made thousands of sales calls and closed many deals. They've survived – not just the career - but likely dozens of managers, companies, mergers, layoffs and more. They've likely been through multiple attempts to change the way they sell and do their jobs through sales training, automation, laptops, you name it. To survive, they've learned to sell their own way and do what's necessary to keep the home office and their managers happy. It's easy to see why they can sometimes be a bit skeptical of new ways of selling.

I suggest you do everything you can to enhance your credibility as a manager. Whatever you do be sure not to abandon the process at the first sign of resistance. Like an unstable, aggressive dog that smells fear, your veteran salespeople will sense quickly your lack of commitment to the initiative. You'll not be able to reclaim this and your credibility will take a hit.

Second, let them know that this process is not about them individually, it's about your district or region or sales team. While you believe it will help each person, you are motivated too by the value it will give to the larger group. For example, back to forecasting. You need one funnel and one funnel process to improve your forecasting accuracy. No one can opt out of the process if you are to forecast for the group effectively.

> **The BuyCycle process helps managers connect with veterans on 'neutral' ground.**

You can use the BuyCycle Funnel™ process with veterans to reach them on neutral ground. Your comments and suggestions about the deals they're working on and sales calls they make can be dismissed when you don't know as much about the account, the people, and even the market as the salesperson does. But using the process lets you promote discovery and challenge assumptions which can get you up to speed fast with some of these sales situations – and impress the salesperson with your 'knowledge'. Your comments are less about your experience and more about what the process leads you to question. You're simply using it to understand the buying cycle better – which is what the salesperson should be doing too.

One of my clients was a sales manager for a medical device company and had a sales veteran and top performer who had his own way of selling. We had trained both the manager and his salespeople but the manager was not buying into using our process for this salesperson. My conversation with him went something like this:

Me: "You seem concerned about getting this salesperson to adopt our selling process."

The manager: "I don't want this salesperson to think I'm trying to change how he sells."

Me: "Do you routinely ride with this rep?"

The manager: "Yes."

Me: "What's your goal when you ride with him?"

The manager: "I just want him to know I'm supporting him."

Me: "How do you support him?"

Manager: "I get things he needs. Remove roadblocks at the home office."

Me: "Anything related to pure selling technique and strategy?"

Manager: "He's been at this for so long he knows what he's doing."

Me: "Do you think he has anything more to learn about selling?"

Manager: "I'm sure he'd admit that he does."

Me: "What do you think?"

Manager: "I'm sure there's something he can learn."

Me: "It might be a little harder to find out what that is for someone with his tenure, isn't it?"

Manager: "It probably is."

The problem I discovered with this manager was that he had no way of talking sales to this salesperson. He was uncomfortable doing it so he avoided it altogether. I convinced the manager first that even his top performers not only needed coaching but also *expected* it from the manager. They might be just as shy about asking for it as this manager was shy about giving it. Second, I showed the manager that using the BuyCycle Funnel™ would enhance his credibility with these salespeople because it simply provided the meeting place, a neutral ground, for a natural conversation about the customer's buying process. Third, I suggested that each sale is unique because the buying cycle is unique with each sale and each sale deserved a unique sales strategy. The best way to accomplish that was to get inside the customer's unique buying cycle for each sale and determine the best strategy for winning it.

It's not about cutting the top performers some slack when it comes to getting them to adopt a new way of selling. I don't think they want any more slack than the next person, but they do want to be treated differently. They demand that managers not waste their time – sometimes these well-intentioned sales process initiatives look like corporate BS to these people. This is reasonable. They deserve to be sold. Each one deserves your full commitment to knowing what makes them uniquely strong and uniquely weak and to know what improvements will make the difference in their selling performance.

Salespeople that Aren't Top Performers

While your non top performing salespeople don't have the same demands as your top performers do they still present with challenges to coaching and developing them. Let's see how you can help with these challenges.

If you're a manager with a lot of selling experience in your industry you might find it tough to get your salespeople to sell a certain way – your way. Your way of selling works for you, and it might even work for your salespeople. The problem is your salespeople have no way of translating how you sell in ways they can understand. Early in my sales career I had a manager who kept trying to get me to sell like him, saying about sales calls *"do it like this."* Problem was I couldn't really <u>see</u> how he was doing it. I didn't have a way to look beyond his style and understand the structure underlying it, as much as I wanted to.

When there's a defined framework or process with terms and meaning it acts as a translator. The process is the language you use to speak to your salespeople.

Less tenured salespeople can struggle to make sense out of all of the variables in a complex deal. All of the players involved in the sale, the lengthy sales cycle, the multiple options for the customer to choose from, as well as options the salesperson has in selling, the competition, all of it can sometimes be overwhelming. When you coach to a process it breaks down all of the variables and complexity into parts they can more easily understand and then act on.

This transfer of knowledge goes both ways. A client of mine, a sales manager for a healthcare company, had been in the job for six months and had been trained in the sales process his company had been using already. He came from a different industry altogether. Among his new salespeople, many had several years of experience with their customers. He didn't fight this disadvantage; rather, he used process to quickly get smarter about the customers. As a result, he gained high credibility quickly with his salespeople and they commented about his being a quick study. They helped him learn, through his process based questioning, and in the process they too learned.

You Coach to a Process

Another use of coaching to the BuyCycle Funnel™ and the 8-Step Process is to help salespeople get out of ruts or overcome dry spells.

When a salesperson hasn't sold something in a while he or she may be tempted to put pressure on the situation and do things he wouldn't normally do. He might get away from patient questioning that normally leads to discovery of needs. He might try to shortcut the process and submit a proposal before he normally would. He might rush to discount for fear of losing the sale. The absence of process leads to this kind of behavior. In many ways this is like trying to control something you have no control over, the outcome.

As a manager, your job is to keep your salespeople focused on what they can control, their sales process. They can control their call planning, their questioning, their intelligence gathering, assessing the players in the buying process, their strategies, and more.

Once you have a framework or process in place there's one key to promoting the right dialogue – it's asking good questions. Let's see how the BuyCycle Funnel™ helps you do this.

Asking Questions is the Key to Good Coaching

Someone once said that it's sometimes better to have the right question than to have the right answer. This is especially true when you have no answer!

But where do the questions come from? It's easy to say it comes from being in the job forever and experience. While there may be some truth to that it doesn't help you as a sales manager managing people who haven't been in the job forever and who don't have experience. It also doesn't help you transfer your own selling acumen and experience to your salespeople, veteran and rookies alike. The questions come from the process.

Promote Discovery and Challenge Assumptions

Remembering that two of your coaching principles is promoting discovery and challenging assumptions you can quickly see that asking questions will determine how well you perform on these two principles. The good news is the process makes it fairly easy to execute on this.

For example, you know that the customer's first stage of the buying cycle is the customer committing to meaningful dialogue and recognizing a problem. Meaningful dialogue helps your salespeople get in early and get a leg up on understanding needs that develop and evolve later. Without it, they might think the customer has a problem, and they might be right. And they might be making some assumptions that will cost them valuable time and position to win the sale later. Here is one of the best ways to keep your salespeople sharp in their questioning. When you're discussing a deal, before it gets too far along the buying process ask the salesperson what constituted meaningful dialogue and what problems did the customer expressly state. There might be time to identify the real needs and motivations and start selling to those.

So how do you get someone to tell you he has a problem? While it might not be easy to admit a problem, people are usually not shy about complaining when something's not right. You simply ask questions to learn about usage, history, application, trends, performance, etc. Once the customer has committed to meaningful dialogue and expressed a problem you've got to understand if he's committed to doing anything about that problem.

- *Is this something that's getting in the way of what you're trying to do every day?*

- *Just how big of an issue is this problem?*

- *I know you've said it's a problem, but I also know it's not likely the only issue you're wrestling with. How does it rank with all of the other issues you're dealing with?*

- *Do you know enough about the problem to be committed to move forward to find a solution?*

- *For others to move forward with a solution of some type do you think we've got enough information for them?*

When the opportunity reaches later stages of the buying cycle the model again becomes the basis for your questions.

For example, another common mistake that salespeople make is identifying the wrong person as the one with financial authority to make a purchase. In Commit Funding, we know that there's usually one person who plays this role, and until this person flips the switch and says spending money to fix the problem is ok the opportunity isn't advancing. The people will have to live with the problem no matter how frustrated some might be.

These are some simple questions to ask your salesperson to answer at this stage:

- *Which person has authority to authorize a purchase?*

- *What makes you say that this person has this authority for this purchase, and hasn't passed that authority on to someone else, or doesn't have to seek someone else's approval for the purchase?*

- *Has this person ever authorized a purchase of this amount before?*

- *Is this person the same as the person who will sign the agreement or purchase order?*

Similarly, for the stage Define Decision Criteria, you'll want to know what the criteria are and who came up with them, so you might ask your salesperson this:

- *Of all the criteria you've uncovered, which ones are the most important to the customer?*

- *What makes you say this?*

- *Why are these the most important criteria to them?*

- *Are they willing to forego getting other things in return for getting these needs resolved?*

Coaching to the BuyCycle Funnel™ will take commitment and passion. It could become the most valuable tool in your bag. As managers, you play a pivotal role in leading change in the way your people sell and manage their funnels. I'm painting a strategic view of the funnel's role in all of this. Your coaching will be more effective when it is within that context.

So it's not just about the funnel, but rather about a funnel process. If you stopped there in your own commitment to adopting this approach you'd be doing great. However, there are some additional ways to further embed the concept of the BuyCycle Funnel™ and the 8-Step Process in your company. Let's see how you can do that.

Part Four:

Broader and Deeper Application of the BuyCycle Funnel™

Chapter 8

Using the BuyCycle Funnel™ with a Customer Facing Selling Method

By now you've seen how the BuyCycle Funnel™ defines the customer's buying process, stage by stage through its decision making, and why it is your guide for selling for the opportunity. It tells you where the opportunity is in that process, what the customer has committed to, and what the customer has to commit to next for the opportunity to move to the next stage. The value of the BuyCycle Funnel™ is clear – by knowing where the opportunity is, you can better decide what selling activities you should do to move it to the next stage. Your selling activities will have greater impact if you follow this sequence.

The BuyCycle Funnel™ helps you know what stage the customer is at in the buying process, but how does that opportunity actually move from one stage to the next? How does the customer actually go from Recognizing a Problem to Defining the Economic Consequence of that problem? Or, from Defining Economic Consequence to Committing Funding, and so on?

> **How does an opportunity advance through the buying process? Someone commits - the customer.**

The answer is someone makes it move. But, not you. *The customer.* Someone at the customer who is participating in the buying process gives this opportunity energy and momentum and life. Someone with enough influence and clout to initiate the process or continue moving it along toward a purchase. Someone willing to make commitments. Someone who believes that there's benefit to himself or herself and to the company – that it's worth the effort to *do something*.

As a salesperson you find yourself in the middle of this every day. The question is how you influence it. That's what this chapter is all about. Your role in moving the sale along. But now you know that 'moving it along' means something different – it's not really the sale, but rather the customer's buying process. While you've heard me preach for seven chapters that the buying process is the key to effective selling, it's not something that has to happen to a customer without you involved - you can have a great deal of influence on it. Customers don't go through buying processes in isolation. Many of them rely on the input from others, including salespeople to help them along their decision path. The more you can influence them the more successful you'll be. Let's see how.

Customer Facing Selling Method

When you think about influencing the customer's buying process you're really influencing the people that participate in it. Where and how do you have an opportunity to influence these people? One place is through the advertising and promoting that your company does. This could be print ads, web ads, trade show presence, direct mail, email campaigns, special events, and anything else that might fall under a marketing category.

The other place is through your direct selling contact with the people. These meetings are your opportunities to persuade each and every stakeholder in the buying process to buy something from you. The way you approach and conduct these sales calls falls under the category of what I'll call a *customer facing selling method*. Your intent is to have a *meaningful dialogue* with these stakeholders throughout the sale, to ask and learn about needs, pressures, fears, objectives, and more, to get commitment, and to show the customer the link between your solution and his or her needs. What you'll learn in this chapter is not a new customer facing method. There are many on the market and some of them are very good. What you'll learn is how to combine your customer facing selling method with the BuyCycle Funnel™ to have maximum impact on influencing the customer's buying process.

To get started, I'll level set a few things about customer facing selling methods. I'll explain the structure behind all of them and explain their intent. Then, I'll show you how understanding the buying process for the *individual* is key to knowing how to use these methods to influence the buying process for the sale, e.g. what the BuyCycle Funnel™ maps to. Finally, you'll see how integrating your customer facing selling method to the BuyCycle Funnel™ stage by stage will let you have the maximum impact on the customer's buying process and get you closer to winning each sale.

A Natural Fit

The BuyCycle Funnel™ and a customer facing selling method naturally go together. Let's see why.

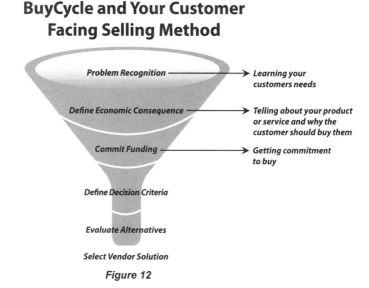

BuyCycle and Your Customer Facing Selling Method

Problem Recognition ──────→ Learning your customers needs

Define Economic Consequence ──────→ Telling about your product or service and why the customer should buy them

Commit Funding ──────→ Getting commitment to buy

Define Decision Criteria

Evaluate Alternatives

Select Vendor Solution

Figure 12

The BuyCycle Funnel™ is a way to understand the customer's buying process for a complex sale and set better sales strategy. The individual buying process is what the individuals are going through as a part of the buying process for the group. Influence the individual and by definition you influence the whole group.

Another key similarity to both buying processes is commitment. For an opportunity to advance, the customer must make commitments. And for the individual to go through his buying process, he must also make commitments. When you align these two with the BuyCycle Funnel™, you've got a powerful tool to be productive in your selling.

'Method' Neutral

The BuyCycle Funnel™ is a method neutral component to your sales process. You can use any other sales method you want with the BuyCycle Funnel™. My own clients have used it with Miller Heiman courses such as Conceptual Selling and Strategic Selling, and with: Solution Selling, Professional Selling Skills, SPIN Selling, and other courses designed by internal trainers and sales leaders.

How Individuals Buy

The answer to how you can influence the buying process is found in understanding the decision making process that individuals go through. After all, people buy, not companies. The more you know about how people buy, the better you'll be at selling and at using the BuyCycle Funnel™. We can help you right now understand that better. Let's review what we know about the decision making process for individuals and see how that is affected when the person goes through that process as part of a group of people making a decision in a company.

Models of Individual Decision Making

In an earlier chapter, I referenced a few well established and research validated models of how people make purchasing decisions. These models help you understand better the decision making process your customers go through and therefore put you in a better position to know how to sell to them. It's not a bad idea to go back and review that to make sure you understand the buying process approach fully.

Buyer Motivation

In all of the models, personal motivations play a role in how decisions get made. Personal motivations are different from the 'business type' motivations such as a need to increase productivity by 10%, or a need to keep SG&A costs at a specific percent of sales. An example of a personal motivation is someone wants a promotion, or wants to be recognized as a real consensus builder. These motivations are usually hard to quantify, but you'd be misguided if you tried. The point is people have very personal, very unique influences affecting their decision making. The more you can uncover and sell to these the more effective you will be.

Just think about your own purchasing patterns and ask a few tough questions. For example, is that car you drive really just transportation? Or do you look pretty cool with the top down and the Bose stereo cranking? Did you need the Dooney & Burke purse, or the Thomas Hardy bracelet, or do you just like the way it makes you feel? How about that John Deere tractor? I know they're well made, but some lesser known brands are pretty well made too, and don't cost nearly as much. What about the $500 golf club? Does it make you feel like you belong, or was it a reward to yourself for all you do for your family and work? Don't get me wrong here. None of this is a judgment on you, or me for that matter; they're observations of our behavior. And when you're trying to learn about someone's needs for the products or services you are selling, the more you know about the personal motivations the better you'll be at selling to them.

Marketing Also Influences the Customer

Marketers use these models to reach and influence consumers. By knowing where the customer is in his decision making process, marketers can influence that process with targeted marketing efforts and messages. For example, if a consumer wasn't thinking she needed a new stereo, and was not in the problem recognition stage, the marketers of stereo equipment could target creating awareness to get her thinking she needs one. If she's not crazy about her current stereo and is reminded about it every time she turns it on, marketers could try to persuade her to take action on that and begin to more seriously consider a stereo purchase. If she's been thinking about buying a stereo but isn't sure what kind to buy, marketers could differentiate their stereo features or capabilities to persuade her to buy a specific brand.

While it's easy to see how direct selling and marketing alone can influence the individual in a business to business selling environment, marketing combined with selling is even more powerful.

> **Marketing could design sales collateral that is targeted to specific stages of the customer's buying process and have a greater impact on influencing it.**

For example, marketing could design sales collateral that is targeted to specific stages of the customer's buying process and have a greater impact on influencing it. I experienced this early in my selling career. I sold for a well known and large pharmaceutical company. We had a drug in the NSAID (non steroidal anti-inflammatory) class that was one of several in that class and unfortunately for us not one that doctors typically put on their top three of prescribed NSAIDS. One of the reasons was it had to be taken four times a day and competed against drugs that were taken once a day or twice a day. It also competed against a popular drug that was perceived as being mild on side effects.

Our product manager designed a clever sales piece that told the doctors when to use our NSAID and when to use our competitors. It said don't use ours when convenience is your number one objective, use competititor A. Don't use ours when mild side effects is your number one objective, use competitor B. But use ours when your number one objective is efficacy. When your patient needs a drug that will really work. We told doctors not only when to use ours but also when to use the competitors. This was the simple, clear message that an army of salespeople delivered. It worked. Our market share increased as a result. The other lesson here is that sales executed well on the marketing strategy.

Business to Business Selling

Do these models of individual decision making apply in the business to business selling environments? You'd better believe they do. Motivations are present and real in any environment of decision making. In Bonoma's Harvard Business Review paper he refers to a 'psychology of buying' that salespeople would be smart to be aware of because salespeople who are good at selling to that psychology can close a higher percentage of sales and avoid the unpleasant surprises that often trip them up. He says of selling corporate jets to executives, there are several decision makers other than the CEO or owner. The board might be involved. Maybe pilots that the CEO uses. Maybe the CFO. They all play certain roles in the purchase. But in selling to the CEO Bonoma says "If you can't find the kid in the CEO, you won't sell him the jet." Imagine inside the CEO's body a little boy who became fascinated with planes and made a promise to himself that one day if he made it big he'd buy one of those planes for himself. Some salespeople might think this is corny or not reasonable, and no way would they sell like that to the CEO of a major company. Honestly, I don't know if it's corny or not, but I do know that reaching the CEO on this level gets to the deep down motivation that he has. Reaching him like that lets him know that you 'get it'. As long as you can satisfy his other needs (size of plane, speed, seating capacity, accessories, etc) you've got the edge over all other sellers that don't get it. Nothing corny about cashing a big commission check is there?

When a person participates in a group buying process it's likely that there are more pressures on that person in the decision process. This person is thinking about how his or her preferences and choice will be perceived by the boss, the direct reports, the colleagues, and others. There's a saying that says the fear of doing something wrong and making a mistake is a stronger motivator than the excitement of the possibility of improving and making something better. And the fear of doing something wrong is such a strong motivator that it sometimes prevents people from changing and doing something right. Most people don't have to look far for validation of this. Some times it's easier to do nothing, to live with the problem you know rather than risk your credibility on making a change.

Personal Motivations Have a Broad Impact on Your Selling Efforts

Personal motivations have a broad impact on your selling efforts at many points along the sale. For example, the reason that an opportunity becomes a lead for you in the first place is due to somebody at the customer having the energy to investigate and explore his situation and give you a call, or take your timely call. He's motivated and inspired more by the personal impact, not the business impact. He didn't wake up saying "today I've got to tackle that productivity issue because my goal is to improve it by 10%." Instead he says, "I've got to tackle that productivity issue because my bonus and that promotion depends on it. My reputation's on the line. If I get the promotion I'll get a raise, and the raise will help me get the country club membership or the new car I've been wanting."

If a sale you've begun becomes stalled, the reason it's stalled goes to a root cause of some person not able to or willing to reverse that. There's no one in the buying process who believes that it's worth his or her personal energy and credibility and reputation to kick start this project and fight for its existence. That's a simple diagnosis, and I don't mean to discount the difficulty of selling into it. But by breaking it down this way, you should be able to set better sales strategy because you'll understand better why it's stalled.

For example, in the retirement services industry, it's sometimes difficult to get someone motivated to switch from one set of funds to another or from one advisor to another advisor. Even when the current funds are not performing well or the advisor has disappeared and doesn't service the account any more. If you're an advisor you might have a great product and excellent track record of servicing clients. If it's a CEO or CFO that needs to be compelled to switch and right now isn't compelled, you might scratch your head in disbelief but the fact is you haven't discovered the deep down, underlying reasons for that complacency. Until you do you won't motivate these people to switch. Your selling efforts need to be aimed at uncovering that motivation.

> **Until you discover - and sell to - the deep down, personal motivation someone has, you'll have a hard time convincing that person to take action.**

I'll add one more thing to this section. Personal motivations are absolutely invaluable to you as you try to get certain people to be on your side and help you win the sale. These 'advocates' are people who are inspired and motivated to help you, for many different reasons. Your task as a salesperson is to find these people, recruit them, and put them to work to help you win new business.

Commitment in Individual Decision Making

In addition to buyer motivation, buyer commitment plays a key part in an opportunity moving from one stage to the next.

It really goes back to an old saying, 'talk is cheap.' If a customer is experiencing some problems, there's no cost to thinking about the problems or how they might be fixed. But when a person commits to acting on the problem that's the stuff of a buying process in motion.

For example, to go from Problem Recognition to Define Economic Consequence takes commitment. In Problem Recognition the person is simply aware. But in Defined Economic Consequence she's taken the time to understand better the cost of the problem. She's invested time perhaps in collecting reports that show cost information. She might have pulled in other people in this effort, which is not only time spent but also credibility spent. She's carved out time in her busy schedule to learn more, and has likely thought of the possibility of where this exploration ultimately might lead – a recommendation to change and go through an evaluation of alternatives to pick the best solution.

One of my clients that sells software would often try to get new prospects to evaluate its software as a way to learn more about it. Seems simple enough, and at no cost what's the problem? The problem is it takes time and it does cost money, and that's the thing executives are constantly fighting to control and stretch. This pilot tactic was not as successful as they had hoped.

Now that we've reviewed how individuals go about the decision making process let's see how a customer facing selling method combined with the BuyCycle Funnel™ can help you influence the sale.

Customer Facing Selling Methods

What is a customer facing selling method? It's simply a method for conducting a meeting with a customer or prospect during the process of trying to sell something. You do it every day. These are the face to face sales calls or even phone to phone calls that you make. Not the routine or even unique visits you have with customers. A sales call is different from these other customer calls mainly because the sales call is largely about getting the customer to commit - at that meeting and eventually later when they buy something from you. And when they enter that context they act differently than when you stop by for any other reason.   Any other type of customer meeting is largely about some commitment that's on your back, like following up with something the customer requested, or putting out a fire for a customer or solving a problem with your product or service.

A sales manager of one of my clients really drove home the distinction with this story. I was speaking at his company's sales conference one year and at dinner that night he said he appreciated the point about sales calls versus other calls that I had made earlier in the day. He said he has let some very good people go – fired – because they didn't get the distinction. They were some of the nicest people he had known. But because they didn't get the difference between getting commitment and otherwise making a visit, he had to let them go. He told me these were some of the hardest decisions he's made as a manager. The rest of the story is that many of these people he let go called him later in their careers to thank him for doing it – they weren't cut out for selling.

Some salespeople are disciplined in the way they approach sales calls, while some are not. Some salespeople have lots of talent for making sales calls and for doing the things that have to be done to be effective. Talent can take these salespeople a long way in their careers. But talent is also part of the problem. Talent will take them only so far. The real sales pros become pros because they are students of their craft and they take the time to understand how they can leverage their talent to get even better, to know what their strengths and weaknesses are, and what they have to do to get to the next level of competency for selling.

How Customer Facing Selling Methods Work

When comparing customer facing selling methods, they all approach the task of making a sales call somewhat differently, but the good ones all share a common intent and structure. First the intent.

Intent

The good customer facing selling methods are out to help you do the following things in your selling:

- Establish your credibility and help you earn the right to have meaningful dialogue with a customer

- Ask questions and do discovery of needs

- Create and expand awareness of needs and discuss consequences of the customer doing nothing

- Develop those needs

- Help the customer create a vision of 'better'

- Tell the customer about features and benefits of the products / services / solutions

- Link your offering to the customer's needs

- Get the customer to commit to taking action

They also approach this task in their own ways and style. Some might have a strong trust angle to them. Others emphasize asking questions. Others require a sequence to be followed to achieve the end result. Some emphasize getting commitment. Some are founded in principles that go back several decades, while others suggest a more modern style that's right for today's selling. For today anyway. Some of them are based on lots of research and study of what good salespeople do when they make sales calls. Some are tailored for certain types of selling environments like banking or insurance or pharmaceutical selling. Some are simply based on one person's experience, albeit in some cases a ton of experience, not just making thousands of sales calls but learning what worked and what didn't.

Structure

The good customer facing methods all share the following kind of structure underlying their methods:

- How to open the meeting

- How to do discovery and learn needs

- How to tell about your products and services

- How to get customer commitment

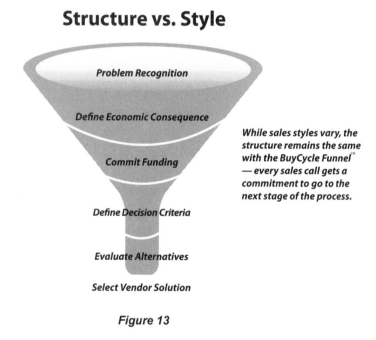

Structure vs. Style

While sales styles vary, the structure remains the same with the BuyCycle Funnel™ — every sales call gets a commitment to go to the next stage of the process.

Figure 13

For the most part, customer facing selling methods work by putting structure to this flow of opening, doing discovery and learning needs, telling about your products and services and why the customer should buy them, and then getting commitment. The structure allows you to be more consistent and effective.

But executing on this structure is only part of the equation for effectively selling.

> **You can make fundamentally solid sales calls by the book so to speak and still lack effectiveness if they're not made in the context of the customer's buying process.**

For example, the customer might drag you in to prepare and present a proposal and you could do a bang up job of that, but what if the customer isn't ready to act on that proposal? You know how I'd coach you – don't do it! The customer should commit to acting on the proposal you'll deliver *before* you deliver it, otherwise you're committing to something that's much more than what the customer is willing to commit to right now. The customer isn't necessarily stringing you along by asking for a proposal. But it's your job to confirm where the customer is in his decision making process – your sales productivity depends on it. Proposals are a big deal. Maybe the customer really needs budget information, not a proposal. You can still meet his needs in other ways and then deliver a proposal later when he's ready to act.

Influencing the Individual

Knowing where the customer is in the buying process helps you set a strategy for selling to each of the individuals that make up that buying process. After all, people buy, not companies. To influence the buying process you've got to influence the individual. To influence the individual you need to know two things. One, where he or she is in his own buying process, and two, where he or she fits in with others in the buying process as a whole.

To be compelled to buy, a person has to first see a problem and see how they affect him or her; but, these problems have to be perceived as problem enough to do something about them. To see this, individuals go through their own buying process, a field of research that has been well documented and studied. For example, why agree to set up a trial or evaluation of your product if you can't find someone with the right kind of influence to agree beforehand to acting in some reasonable way within some reasonable period of time on the information he or she will discover as a result of the evaluation? If the evaluation will not move this person forward in his decision making process it's a good chance that the evaluation is a waste of your time. Maybe there's someone else with influence who sees the evaluation in a different light and how it will help him or her personally get closer to the bottom of the problems he has been experiencing. It's possible the customer still wants an evaluation done, and that's ok, but it should probably come later in the buying process. And yet, salespeople offer trials and evaluations and samples all the time without getting customer commitment.

All of this happens at the moment of truth – standing face to face with the customer and making some assessment of what's the next best thing the seller can do to help move this person along his buying process. Knowing where they are in that process is your first focus, and then figuring out the best thing to do to move the customer further along is your next.

Applying Customer Facing Methods to the BuyCycle Funnel™

So how do you use a customer facing sales method with the BuyCycle Funnel? Well, think of what you're doing with the BuyCycle Funnel. You're documenting where a customer is in his decision making process and trying to convince the customer to go to the next stage. A customer facing selling method helps you do both.

Confirming where the customer is in the buying process is about looking for tangible evidence. If you've found it, you're making sure it still exists. Sales cycles can be long and the people participating in them can change their minds over time about how they feel about the situation and how it's affecting them.   Use your customer facing selling method to answer the following questions at each stage, throughout the entire cycle:

- What stage is the customer at in his buying process and what tangible evidence is there that he is at that stage?

- What has to happen for the customer to get to the next stage?

- How can I help the customer along his process?

Let's look at this stage by stage.

Pre-Problem Recognition

Before a prospect recognizes a problem, you might label the prospect a Target Account. These are the accounts that are way above the top of your funnel, that you are focusing selling attention on, hoping to discover new sales opportunities. You'd be smart to focus your selling efforts on certain accounts that might present a better match to your knowledge or skills sets or that represent for other reasons a good opportunity for you.   This is a strategic approach to your selling and can pay off in many ways. For one, your close rate will likely be higher for opportunities where there's a great fit to what you do well.   Two, your cost of sales might be lower, especially if these are referrals from satisfied clients.   Three, your sales cycle might be shorter because of higher credibility or other attribute you have. This also reduces your cost of sales. These accounts haven't 'hit' your funnel yet because there's no sales opportunity identified.

How to Influence At This Stage

To influence the customer at this stage you have to either find someone who acknowledges a problem, or help someone recognize a problem. Do you go in and start asking people if they have any problems? Not really. A better angle is to get to know their situation as well as you can. Not only will you find problems that way but you'll also understand them better and faster. This will give you credibility, which you'll need to gain insight and ultimately convince certain people to act on the information you're uncovering. There are many ways to get to know the situation better but it really starts with asking good questions. Here are a few:

- Could you tell me about this system and how you use it?

- Why do you use it that way?

- How does this part of the business affect this other department in work flow?

- Do you have any opinions about people? Process?

- Are the skills that were necessary to succeed in the present environment sufficient to succeed in the direction you want to go? What makes you say that?

- Could you tell me about the processes you use and how effective you believe they are?

- What are your near term goals and objectives? What are the leading indicators you use to track progress toward those goals and objectives?

- Are these stretch goals or ones that are conservatively set?

- What kinds of things have you identified as possible obstacles to achieving the goals and objectives?

It's quite possible you won't find a problem even when you focus on the situation. On a recent sales call I made, following up on a referral from a client, I continued to ask questions about sales strategy, direction, goals, issues, perceived problems, and more to uncover the problems. The person I met with basically came up empty – he said things were going great. So I asked him why he agreed to met with me (thank goodness by phone) and he said he's always looking for new things. People don't buy my services because they're looking for new things. Rather, they have business problems to solve. Right now, he had none that I could uncover and I told him so. I'll stay in touch with him and perhaps I'll be the first one he thinks of when his situation changes.

Be Genuinely Interested and Show the Customer Patience

One of the keys to influencing this stage as a salesperson is to be genuinely interested in his or her situation. It helps to be curious and to want to learn. The more you can get the customer to share with you what his or her environment is like, for him or her personally, the more insight you'll have and the more likely you'll know if a problem exists.

One of my clients is a salesperson who sells into the pediatric and neonatal intensive care units. He sells a sophisticated product to a very intelligent group of customers that ranges from doctors to administrators to nurses to technicians. He makes it policy to know that environment better than any of his competitors. He'll routinely invest a day or so of his own time to accompany one of the doctors or techs throughout the day to get a closer view of their world and their issues. He does this because he's genuinely interested in the people he sells and services, but he also learns of new applications for his product. Think of the credibility this approach gives him.

Paint a Vision of Better

There's a saying 'you don't know what you don't know' that can be relevant for this stage of the customer's buying process. The individual might think everything is fine because he or she is not able to see that there is a better place to be. Your job is to help the customer visualize the possibilities for something better. You do this in a number of ways.

Blue Sky questions. Some clients are receptive to you asking them to think big picture or get into *'what if there were no constraints to resources or money'* kind of dialogue. They like getting out of the day to day focus even if for a few moments while talking with you. Out of these conversations you might uncover some problems. An example of a blue sky question is *"Let's fast forward one year. What are your customers saying about your company? Or, what is the marketplace saying? What are your competitors saying about your company's performance?"* Or, it might be process or work flow related so you can ask *"Describe what a perfect system might look like."*

Share best practices. Customers are often too busy to know what's going on outside of their own world, including how their peer companies are performing or how the best companies in any industry run their businesses so well. You increase your value to customers when you bring these ideas and best practices to them especially to senior executives who are expected to know how their companies compare to others. As a way to get the contact thinking of a better place, you can share with him or her case studies or articles or industry information about a business process or success story.

There's one question or approach I'm reluctant to ask when the customer cannot think of any problems because I think it's a copout to my responsibility to the customer. It goes something like this: *"I know that you're doing many things right with your operation. Is there anything you'd like me to help you do better?"* What's the typical customer answer? *"Look – there's always room to improve."* Which is really saying, you've just asked me a shallow question. I think you risk damaging your credibility. Most of the time they won't bite – they say they're fine and you've bought yourself a one way ticket to the front door.

If you're successful in finding a problem or two during this stage your focus has to be to get the customer to acknowledge it. You simply present what you see to the customer and ask her if she sees the same thing. If she acknowledges it, you've got Problem Recognition. That's an important start to getting the sales opportunity ball rolling, and there's a whole lot more work to be done to get to the next stage.

Problem Recognition Stage

The tangible evidence that the customer has reached Problem Recognition stage is simply the acknowledgment by the customer that there's a problem. So what's your focus at this stage and how can you use a customer facing selling method to influence that? Your focus is to learn as much as you can about the problem, help the customer see the consequences of doing nothing about it, and then try to influence the customer to commit to doing something about it.

Asking Questions

A good customer facing selling method has asking questions as a backbone of the method. But now you can use the BuyCycle Funnel™ to ask better, more pointed questions for each stage of the buying process. For example, at Problem Recognition, you know one thing for sure – the contact in front of you has expressed a problem. That's a start. But what more would you like to know? Here are a few ideas:

- *How long has the problem been going on?*

- *Is it getting worse or better or staying the same? And what makes you say that?*

- *Do other people have the same impression of the problem?*

- *Who doesn't care about it or doesn't think it's a problem? How much does that person's influence count?*

- *What is the buying process you'd go through to learn more, to evaluate, to decide to do something and then select a solution?*

- *Has anything been done to try to fix it? What's been tried? How effective was that?*

- *(Or) What's the reason that nothing has been done to try to fix it?*

- *Who else is the problem affecting and how?*

- *What would he or she say about the problem and how much it's affecting personal or department performance or even credibility?*

- *What's the cost of this problem and is that acceptable? Is there someone who would not accept that?*

- *What's one way we might find out a little more to help you decide the best thing to do about it?*

I'm not suggesting you ask all of these questions. You certainly wouldn't ask all of them on one sales call without irritating the customer. The answers will help you understand things better and decide how to proceed.

Finding People with High Influence to Give Energy to the Opportunity

In a B2B selling environment there are almost always multiple people involved in the buying process. You'll want to find the people with high influence as quickly as you can because they're the ones who have the most say and they influence others. They might be the spark that ignites the opportunity too – the thing that gives it life and momentum. In many ways, without their participation and even endorsement of the problem your selling efforts will have limited or no effect. Your questions and discovery should be directed at learning who these people are. For example, one question you can ask is "of all the people this problem affects, who would most likely want to do something about it? Why is that?" This person might have a personal stake in better performance. You could also ask, "if many people said we should go forward with a solution, who is the one person who could vote no and kill the deal?"

I can't stress enough how important it is to identify these players as quickly as you can. I've seen many a client spend too much time selling to the people who don't have the authority or enough influence to initiate or advance a sale. I'm not saying the opinions of these people don't count. They just don't have the horsepower to muscle their way through the organization to sponsor change. And that's what you need at this stage of the customer's buying process. People who are motivated and authorized to change.

Look for Signs of Personal Gain

Since it takes a lot of energy for someone to eventually conclude that changing is worth the effort you'll want to look early and often for signs of personal gain for the people you're selling to. If you find someone who is new to a position this person might have strong motivations to do something about the problems identified. Addressing problems might be the reason he or she was given the job or the assignment. You have a good excuse to learn about the personal motivations behind that person getting into that position. This will give you a peek at the things on his or her mind. For example, if he was promoted, you might ask, "I'm sure you plan to be in this position as long as it's necessary to accomplish your goals. Is there a legacy or a mark you want to leave when you're ready to move to the next challenge?" Or, "Have you been able to identify the real obstacles yet to better performance here?"

Build Trust and Credibility

Good sales courses emphasize building credibility and trust as early as possible with a new prospect. Of course, you'll want to be building and enhancing credibility throughout the sales process with each and every buying influence involved, but the earlier you build credibility the faster you'll have deeper insight into the customer's situation, problems and intentions for resolving their issues.

Beyond the obvious benefits of establishing trust, it opens up the customer to share insight with you. You'll need this insight to understand his situation better and eventually identify problems. It's one example of tangible evidence when the customer shares more and more information with you about his or her situation.

One of the ways of building trust and credibility early in the discovery is to be prepared completely for the meeting. It shows respect for the person's time and importance. Another way is to tell the customer about yourself and your company and how you approach new prospects. A quick elevator speech with a professional brochure or brief sales literature can make a big impact. You're looking for a fit between the two firms as much as they are looking for it. If you were referred to the customer by someone else you've done business with, leverage that in your opening and throughout the call. Be careful to not let the specifics of your business relationship dominate this call however. It's possible the prospect could say *"we don't have the same selling issues here that she has, and therefore I don't see how we could use you."*

Learning as much as you can about the customer's situation hopefully exposes enough for the customer to stay engaged with you in learning more. And committing to the next step in his buying process - Define Economic Consequence.

Define Economic Consequence

What tangible evidence is there that the customer has reached Define Economic Consequence stage and how can you influence this stage?

The tangible evidence here is hearing the customer speak about the dollars and cents that this problem is costing. A problem that costs the company money gets attention and is nearly always easier to justify spending time and money on than problems that don't. They might describe it as a higher expense or lost revenue. They might call it a productivity problem. At this stage this problem has broken through the noise barrier. Now the executives are looking for additional reasons to keep giving it attention and possibly money to correct it.

How does the customer get this information that a problem is costing money? It might be from daily or weekly reports from the plants or the field. Some companies have special programs that reward employees for identifying cost saving and productivity enhancing opportunities. It could be from an employee who is affected by this problem and has taken the time to do some investigation into it. It might also be from you - a salesperson or account manager doing some assessment of the customer's situation.

How Can You Influence

Your selling efforts should help the customer see the cost of doing nothing. Remember, not all problems get funded. Contributing to a business case not only helps them see the cost and the payoff, it helps you be seen in a very positive way. And since people often choose to live with problems, you've got to inspire the right people to take action on this problem.

Define Economic Consequence doesn't mean that the customer has gone through an extensive analysis of the situation and has concluded what the actual costs are to the problem. It means they've learned important economic things about the situation. In many businesses a detailed business justification isn't necessary for the customer to get to the Commit Funding stage. What is necessary is for the customer to have *enough* information to justify committing funding. In other businesses it feels as though it is necessary to go through this extensive analysis before the customer commits funding but our client experience suggests that that detailed analysis happens later in the customer's buying process, Define Decision Criteria.

For example, one of our clients sells a software solution to agencies in the behavioral health marketplace. The funding that's required to buy six figure software solutions often comes directly from a grant or public monies. Before spending that kind of money the agency needs to have a pretty good idea of the cost of the solution, but what it really needs is a cost of the problem – that is, the cost of not having better software and processes to manage its business. My client plays an important role for the customer at this stage. They can get the client budget type information about a possible solution, which is not as detailed as a proposal. They can also help the client put together the business case that shows cost benefit, not just cost to a solution. We've advised them to tread this path carefully, since creating a business case for the customer can be a big selling investment. They need to get commitment ahead of time that the client is genuinely interested in using the business case to commit to the next step, as long as it gives them the information they need to do that. With the business case, the client seeks approval to spend that kind of money on a software purchase. If they are granted the go ahead, then they've reached Commit Funding and they have to continue evaluating alternatives and eventually select a solution.

The key thing to remember here is that not all problems get funded. Your influence in the sale needs to be aimed at helping the customer decide to fund this problem that will turn into a sales opportunity for you once that occurs. How do you do that? Be sure you tell it to the right person, the person who is authorized to spend the money. In many complex sales there's one person who has the authority to allow a purchase of something to take place. Your task is to find out who would have the authority for the level of purchase for your type of solution, get to that person and hear her or him say she's prepared to spend money to if it comes to that to fix the problems she's been made aware of.

Finding this person is not always easy. Getting someone at the account to help you with this can be invaluable.

Using Someone at the Account to Help You Sell

Often, the person who needs to be sold will rely on close direct reports to come to a decision. If you enlist the support of someone like that your message has a better chance of getting through. Your influence then is more effective if you direct it through this advocate and to the end user who you're really trying to sway. The advocate might suggest she could be your messenger, but I'd resist this and give her a good reason why. The reason is this: there's no one better than you to completely represent your solution and your capabilities. You want to be the one looking that person in the eye and convincing him or her you're the person to get the job done. If this advocate can help you get face to face with the person of authority, then great. If not, you take what you can get.

Bottom line is this: Making a change is usually a big deal for the people you are calling on. Not all problems get funded. Living with the problem can often be a safer choice. You can't make money when that's the choice.

Commit Funding

What tangible evidence is there that the customer has reached Commit Funding stage and how can you influence this stage of the process?

Brief review and reinforcement of this stage: Commit Funding is not giving you an order. It's the customer, through the authority of the one person who is authorized to spend the money, saying we'll genuinely consider making a change. Remember what this person says:

I've seen enough or heard enough of the problems, I realize doing something about them could cost me money and I'm ok with that.

The tangible evidence here can sometimes be very obvious. You might know the person who can authorize spending money to fix the problem and they tell you they've authorized it. Wonderful. It's full speed ahead though you still have a lot of selling to do to win the sale. For example, for one of my clients she has direct access to the president of one of her clients. That president approached her recently and asked her for help with a business problem. It was a modestly sized opportunity for my client and the president confirmed he has money and is ready to spend it. She'll put a proposal together and deliver it directly to the president who will make the decision.

Sometimes it's not so obvious. You might not know who this person is. You might know but you can't get to him or her. You're relying on an advocate at the account to feed you information and give you insight. For many of my clients getting to this person in their sales efforts is one of the most challenging parts of their jobs. We brainstorm ways to get that access, but I also suggest that they should seek the help of others in the account. This opens new paths. Sometimes, my clients are better off using someone else to deliver their messages to these people rather than trying to get to the person with authority at all costs.

How do you influence the buying process at this stage? One, the customer has committed funding, but executives might want to know more about the true cost of the problem or consequence of doing nothing. You can offer to help. Your expertise should be in helping companies like this one understand better its situation so it can make better decisions on what to do. One way to contribute is to offer to the sponsor your time in working with his or her staff to keep things moving ahead and to collect the right information. Two, continue to help the executives feel good about where they are – at commit funding. Just because they reach that stage doesn't mean they can't change their minds. Three, continue helping the customer see what a solution should include. Their next step is to identify the criteria that makes up their set of needs and requirements. Use your credibility to tell them what requirements should be included. Show them how other companies do it.

Decision Criteria Defined

What tangible evidence is there that the customer has reached Decision Criteria Defined stage and how can you influence this stage of the process?

What you're looking for here is evidence that the customer is able to tell you clearly what it's looking for. Specific needs and requirements that have been collectively agreed upon by the group. Even if one or two players have largely shaped the overall requirements. It's possible that there's a requirements document somewhere that can be shared with you. There might be an RFP or RFQ that you can request. The question is what can you do at this stage to influence the customer's decision criteria?

First, if you're coming into the sale at this stage you're behind the game. If the customer has an RFP or even an informal set of requirements defined and you weren't helping them come up with that then you're competing with two possible options. One, some other company that's been helping the customer write the RFP, or two, the customer's own efforts at determining on its own what it needs and what the solution looks like. Either way, you're not in a good position.

Second, the customer's criteria has been shaped by all of the things that have occurred leading up to this stage. This isn't hard to imagine but it will help you think about it for a second. The players have gone through Problem Recognition and Define Economic Consequence and Commit Funding and that whole experience has been fueled by the individual motivations of the players. It's likely that some of them feel stronger about the need to change than other players. Some might have more interest in changing and have a lot on the line regarding personal gain and credibility. As they've gone through their buying process their awareness of the issues became greater the more they understood their situation and the more they believed what was at stake, individually. Bottom line is they've collectively decided to no longer live with the problem. The solution to their own individual needs is like a hole filled with wet concrete – it's setting fast. Soon, there will be no time available to change their minds.

If you're entering the customer's buying process at this stage you might want to *disqualify* this opportunity, as strange as this might sound. You have to take the attitude, privately, that the customer has to prove to you that it is genuinely giving you a shot at its business. Otherwise you have a high risk of being proposal fodder for a company that's moving decidedly down a path of working with another supplier.

How do you disqualify it? Use the BuyCycle Funnel™ how it's intended.

> **Beware of committing to something they ask you to commit to without them committing to something you know is reasonable.**

They might ask you to respond to the RFP they're using. But how can you put forth a good reply to the RFP when you're information deprived? They might disagree. They'll tell you that everything you need to know is on the RFP and this is the way they want to play – with you. You should resist. At a minimum you'll want to learn a lot about how they arrived at the needs identified on this RFP. Those needs belong to people, and those people have something at stake in this buying process. You need to know what's important to several people perhaps, especially the highly influential ones. They might resist and tell you to contact one person with any questions who speaks for the group. She'll tell you what she can while making it fair to all others competing for the business too.

I'm not saying you should not choose to play in these types of sales. Some of you that sell in an environment that's heavily characterized by RFPs live with this all the time. The earlier you can get in front of these sales opportunities the better. When you can't, just realize what you're getting yourself into.

Asking the Right Questions

You'll want to ask questions that get to the heart of your real chance at the opportunity. Here are some standard ones you can modify if they're not in your playbook already:

We're delighted to be invited to earn your business and help you accomplish important objectives. Since we haven't been part of your discovery and problem recognition and consequences and such, we'll be at a disadvantage in responding to the RFP. It'll be important for us to learn first hand from the people who contributed to the RFP, what's important to them and why. We're willing to make that investment of our time. How can we go about setting up those interviews?

We're under no illusion that we're coming into this opportunity at a point where you've decided what you need and why (RFP). That's our fault, not your's. Still, for us to compete we'd like to know a couple of things if you don't mind:

What is it that you see in us that you don't see in the suppliers you're currently evaluating?

Or, what don't you see in the suppliers you're evaluating that you see in us?

Their response is sometimes predictable.

"We can't really do that (give you access to people at this point). It wouldn't be fair to the other suppliers."

"(In inviting you) We're just making sure we consider all of the options."

"Your company comes highly recommended. We are serious about considering your proposal."

"There's nothing really specific. We just want to see what you have. If you don't want to bid then that's your choice."

There's another good reason to come across to the customer this way during the sale. How they respond to your commitment-driven style during the sale is an indication of how they'll act toward you once you have the business. If you don't like the way they respond this business might not be a good fit for you.

Evaluate Alternatives

What tangible evidence is there that the customer has reached Evaluate Alternatives stage and how can you influence the buying process at this stage?

Tangible evidence at this stage is sometimes a closing of the RFP process. The customer gives you a deadline for responding, and cuts off all correspondence after that time. They can be pretty strict with this in some situations. The focus for the customer is evaluating what's in front of them, which is often your proposal. How you deliver that proposal is what I'd like to focus on.

First, a proposal is a formal answer to a defined set of needs, or criteria. You're saying with the proposal here is how we will solve the needs you've expressed.

Second, a proposal should be seen as another point of dialogue between you and the customer. Don't look at it as it's the end of the selling. Although it suggests that the customer is done identifying needs, you can still use the proposal to further the dialogue and help the customer get closer to resolution. By offering two or three different ways to answer the customer's needs, it's possible that the customer picks elements of each offer and combines them to create another one. That's being creative and focused on trying to find a solution.

Three, a proposal doesn't sell itself. It can't walk and talk and emphasize certain points. Therefore you should never send a proposal and expect it to sell for you. Proposals often take hours to prepare and sometimes days. The least the customer can do is take some time to review it with you.

And finally, for the proposal to have the right kind of impact you need the right people in the room reviewing it. Make sure they know this when you set up the review meeting.

Select Vendor Solution

What tangible evidence is there that the customer has reached the Select Vendor Solution stage and how can you influence this stage?

The evidence is usually that the customer has closed the door to any further meetings and dialogue following your proposal delivery and presentation. They believe they've seen what they needed to see and now it's up to them to make a decision.

In most businesses, once the players reach this stage there's not a lot of selling that can be done. You've represented your solution and capabilities and hopefully made a strong connection between the customer's needs and your solution. The minds are often made up by this point. The rest of the buying process is a formality of awarding and executing the deal with the winning supplier.

So what's a salesperson to do to influence this stage? A lot of what you can do is more about what *not* to do. It's tempting to call and email and inquire during this period which for some of you and your business environments can be a long time. It's important to be patient and avoid doing things that can hurt you. It's best if you have one contact on the inside like an advocate who you can call to see if he or she has heard of anything, but even with this person you don't want to come across as being too eager.

Contract or Purchase Order Signed

At this stage, the customer has contractually committed. It's in writing. You've officially made a sale. Congratulations.

Is the selling over? For the opportunity, absolutely. It's important that that point be made to signal the finality of the sale. In some environments the selling might be over, but the work isn't necessarily done. Many of my clients have sales environments where closing the sale isn't so cleanly defined by a contract or PO being signed. They have other defining kinds of events that indicate to them that a sale has been made such as the product is shipped, or it gets stocked on the shelf, or there's a new standing order in place with an initial order being placed. The focus shifts from getting to the close to promoting and maintaining a heightened awareness that the product is now available, or to a post sale implementation schedule of tasks that the salesperson plays a role in completing.

Summary

The BuyCycle Funnel™ pinpoints where the opportunity is in the customer's buying process, but it's the one on one discovery and persuasion and getting commitment from each person participating in that process that moves the opportunity along the BuyCycle. Having a BuyCycle Funnel™ leverages the effectiveness of your customer facing selling method. And having a good customer facing selling method leverages the effectiveness of your BuyCycle Funnel™. Combining these two elements makes for a powerful selling approach. Master it and your sales productivity will increase, you'll sell more, and you'll be more efficient.

Chapter 9

Applying the BuyCycle Funnel™ to Strategic or National Accounts

Many of my clients have engaged me over the years to help them sell to customers that are large, or strategic to their business, sometimes global, but always significant and complex to sell to. These are customers where the client usually has a base of business already and they're trying to protect it or grow it. This type of business falls into a category that is commonly referred to as strategic or key accounts, or national accounts. This business is especially important either because it represents a large percentage of the client's overall revenue or profits, or it is strategically important to the client for non-revenue reasons – or both. One of the best ways to protect and grow the business at these accounts is to create a funnel management process for them. In this chapter, I'll show you why you might want to do that for these customers and show you how to make the BuyCycle Funnel™ a core part of your sales and customer management processes for these accounts.

> Since national and strategic account revenue is so important, having a funnel management process is a smart investment.

Defining Strategic Accounts and National Accounts

While strategic and national accounts share common characteristics, they are different in many ways. Since these differences require unique selling approaches and unique approaches to funnel management, let's start by defining these two types of accounts.

Strategic Accounts

Strategic or key accounts are accounts that are best defined by Mr. Noel Capon, professor of business at Columbia University's Graduate School of Business, in his book Key Account Management and Planning. He's authored many books on management and consults with corporations throughout the world. In selecting and defining a strategic or key account, Capon says that companies should select accounts "that are truly important for long-run organizational health." He suggests that this means the company meets one or more of three major criteria:

1. The company represents significant revenue and/or profits to the supplier.

2. The company is valued by the supplier as being a very good cultural fit and one that fits the supplier's higher level strategic direction and strategy.

3. The company indirectly impacts the supplier's sales and profits.

For example, if you have an account that represents 12% of your sales, that's a lot of revenue resting with one company. You'd likely want to treat it as a strategic account and do everything you can to protect that revenue. You might have extra people assigned to the account, or give the account faster and easier access to your technical or other resources. You might have special equipment or technology purchased just for this account.

Some accounts are strategic because your company has more than one division selling to it. You might decide to approach the account from a high level that crosses not only all of their divisions, but *yours* too. When you have a lot of business across multiple divisions of the customer, it's reasonable for them to expect you to recognize that and take steps to make it easier and more efficient to interact with and do business with your company. This requires special investments and well-thought out planning and committed execution to make that possible. And because it requires investments it should be worth the effort.

Capon says that you'll want to clearly identify the accounts that are strategic or national. There are many ways to do this, but it simply means you define a set of criteria to 'screen' the accounts for inclusion or not. Criteria could include number of locations, number of employees, management style, degree of partnering, degree of innovation, focus on quality or other performance measures, public or private ownership, and many others. The key is to apply the criteria and be disciplined about acting on what the information tells you. With no disciplined approach you might miss out on developing some very lucrative relationships and business with accounts that are a good fit, or you might invest too much time and resources in accounts that won't return to you sales and profits you'd need for your investment in them.

National Accounts

A different category of accounts that you'll want to put a funnel process to is your national accounts. These accounts are those that typically require a contract or an agreement as a condition for doing business. These companies often have multiple locations or facilities or branches around the country or even the world. All or many of these locations might use a given supplier's products or services, and so it makes sense for them to try to establish contracts with the suppliers to secure availability, get consistent pricing, or secure predictable terms and conditions. They can also expect to get preferential pricing or other treatment when they pool their purchasing across multiple locations and facilities. The suppliers selling to national accounts often have salespeople located locally or regionally calling on the sites or facilities or branches. These salespeople might have dozens or even hundreds of accounts they call on in their respective territories, not just the local locations for the national accounts. We'll see later in the chapter that coordinating the selling efforts of the national account teams and the field salesforce is key to maximizing the effectiveness of the national accounts group.

One example of a national account scenario is with manufacturers of medical equipment and supplies selling to hospitals. The manufacturers commonly sell into a contract environment, sometimes lead by what's called a group purchasing organization (GPO). The GPO is a third party entity that sits between the supplier and the hospital. It gets contracts signed on behalf of its member hospitals. The hospital joins the GPO and pays it a fee for membership. In return the GPO secures contracts with manufacturers. For example, if you're a hospital and you buy $15M of IV solutions each year you'd expect your GPO to get you special terms and pricing on those purchases. So it goes with all of the products your hospital uses. If you're the GPO and you have forty five of these hospitals as members you can take some heavy leverage to the manufacturers to seek special pricing and terms for just this one product category. Add to that the many other product categories and you get a picture of the size of the purchasing at stake. If you're the manufacturer of the solutions, you'd be very interested in having a contract with all forty five of those hospitals. You'd probably be willing to give up something in return for that kind of access.

One thing that complicates the contracting in this hospital purchasing environment is when the hospitals purchase off of the contracts that their GPOs have secured. Although the GPO isn't too happy about their members doing that, because it can undermine the position of the GPO if it happens a lot, it's part of the game.

Contracting like this at a national level for local and regional sites and facilities also occurs in other industries such as the financial services industry and the home building trade. Companies that sell retirement products (called providers) seek to secure agreements with their channels (brokerage firms and advisors). A given brokerage firm like Raymond James or UBS might have thousands of advisors selling retirement services or other investment products and might have agreements with half a dozen different providers and the funds and services they provide. If you're the provider of the retirement product in this chain you obviously want your funds to be the first or maybe second choice among those half dozen. Your salespeople on the street are calling on the channel at the local level and trying to keep that first or second place position, or get there.

For a supplier selling to national home builders, it might seek national contracting with builders so that the supplier's salesforce can call on local and regional offices and earn the business one project or one development at a time. Like the hospital and retirement services businesses, there might be a dual source arrangement that doesn't guarantee that the supplier will get the business. Its field salespeople are required to call on the local offices to earn business at the local level.

The Need for a Process Where It Counts the Most

In most companies that have strategic or national accounts, this business gets a lot of attention from management because it typically comprises a sizeable percentage of the company's overall sales or profits. If that's not reason enough, these accounts might give suppliers a desired position in an industry and class of customer that helps you sell to more customers in that industry. For example, a client of mine sells to Wal-Mart, the biggest fish in the retail pond. Besides being the biggest dollar revenue account that my client has, it's also a high profile account because of Wal-Mart's number one position in the retail industry. For the past few years we've put funnel management processes to how this account is being managed and have helped the client make significant strides towards growing its business and being more productive about the business it wins.

Well managed companies understand the value of investing in business processes for these accounts. Processes put the proper spotlight on the importance of the accounts. They help the supplier understand the true strengths and weaknesses of the relationship, which lets them avoid surprises and get the most from its investments of people and resources. There's often a lower cost to selling to these accounts since you've already got a relationship established. You know their needs and problems. You might know their markets and their customers. You should know how they use your product and why. You know their buying processes. All of these things take an incredible amount of time to gather. It's good business to protect this investment and leverage it to sell additional products and services.

One of my clients understands this well. They're a large enterprise selling healthcare management solutions to hospitals and clinics. Of the several hundred accounts they sell to about fifty represent just over half of the company's overall revenue. A few years ago management recognized this and set about putting process to protecting its position. First, it got the salesforce focused on selling even more to these accounts, growing its share within the accounts and enjoying better margins in the process. They put process to its selling efforts, training and coaching the hundreds of salespeople to analyze their opportunities and work the sale within a specific framework. Finally, we also designed and implemented a sales funnel management process for these accounts. The payoff? They've documented an increase in sales in these accounts of over three times the increase in sales in other accounts.

(The not so obvious need for) A Sales Funnel Process

Getting a lot of attention doesn't always translate into getting the right kind of attention for strategic and national accounts. Despite the cost of lost revenue or profits from losing an account like this, surprisingly few suppliers have invested in sales funnel processes for them. This is misguided since the goal over time of your strategic and national account efforts must be to grow the business, not simply manage the account and the current business you have. If you don't grow sales in these accounts, some day you won't have anything to manage.

Capon agrees. He says, "Over the years I have become more and more convinced of the importance of this approach to managing the sales force." I suspect that the reason that more companies haven't done this is similar to the reasons that companies haven't made a similar funnel investment in their main business. It's a combination of lack of awareness, lack of focus in the trade, and misunderstanding of what a funnel can do for a business. Without a conscious investment in funnel management with these accounts, some of you could be putting your most important business at risk. Having a funnel process ensures that it is getting the right kind of selling attention.

Selling Challenges with Strategic and National Accounts

To know how to design and implement a sales funnel process for these accounts you need to recognize first that there are unique selling challenges for this part of your business. They require slightly different selling approaches and also slightly different funnel strategies.

Having a Selling Focus in Strategic Accounts

One challenge that deserves the first attention is perhaps the one that's not so obvious in needing attention – the need to have a *selling* mentality for your strategic and national accounts.

One reason this might not be obvious could be due to the kind of business you're getting in the accounts. For example, if you're a food service supplier and you win a multi year contract to provide services to the local school district's junior high and high schools, the contract is for defined services to be paid at a defined fee. It's all spelled out at the inception of the contract. You might be able to upsell some services along the way but maybe not a significantly higher amount. Your focus is to service the account well enough to put you in good position to renew the contract when it expires years later.

But even with other types of accounts where there's plenty of opportunity to grow the business once you have it, it's sometimes not obvious to the supplier that they should be doing that.

In the strategic account reviews I've done with clients over the years one fairly common theme I've noticed is that they sometimes confuse all of the support and management and servicing of the account with selling. Simply, selling is the task specific stuff you do in searching for net new business. It's the stuff that has the most direct impact on uncovering and qualifying net new business. For example, if a client is using a particular product of yours and you believe that it could get an even better result in performance if it also used a service you sell with that product, you've got to isolate the service opportunity for what it is, a new sales opportunity. You might have to raise the issue and create awareness, show them the economic benefit, and get a purchase order signed. Some of you might say this is obvious, and you might be right. But I hope you don't think that these new sales opportunities just pop up and the selling takes care of itself as long as you're doing a great job of servicing and managing the account. The opportunities are often there, but without an active selling frame of mind among your account staff don't be surprised if these opportunities never develop.

It's also tempting to say that taking good care of the existing business is selling because the account won't be eager to discuss new business opportunities with you if you don't first take care of what you have. Don't talk yourself into this and be mislead. The aforementioned is necessary, but don't confuse good servicing with selling. If you've ever lost a strategic account and truly did a wonderful job of servicing and taking care of the people and the business, then you know what I'm saying. Someone came in and sold the account and took it right out from under you despite your acceptable or even impressive account management.

One thing I've initiated with my clients in these account reviews is to set aside completely separate time for focused discussion of new sales opportunities. By putting a spotlight on net new business we first raise awareness. Then we set strategies. The next step is of course committing to a funnel process.

Role Conflict for Account Manager

A second challenge has to do with the role shift of the primary account manager or salesperson for the account. This situation is more common among strategic accounts than with national accounts. What happens is the seller helps get the business and then finds herself or himself being required to spend more time servicing and managing than selling. They not only have less time to sell to this account, but they also have less time to sell to other accounts.

In other situations, a super salesperson like the CEO or VP of Sales for a company acts as a rainmaker to bring in new strategic or key business. Once the business is closed the supplier assigns a person as the account manager, sometimes locating that person at the customer's offices. This person is asked to play primarily an account management role, but later the supplier's executives try to get the account manager to step up his or her selling activities and uncover new business in the account. There's nothing inherently wrong with this – you just need to be aware of the skill set of the account manager and how equipped he or she is to play a dual role. With good account management and selling processes you can pull it off.

Many Touch Points on the Account

Accounts that get a lot of attention often have many people in different departments touching these customers. This presents challenges to managing the selling process.

For example, a lead might be uncovered by an inside salesperson during a routine checkup call to the customer. Inside sales hands off the lead to the field salesperson who has to follow up. The more that the salesperson knows about the lead the better strategy he or she will have. After the salesperson follows up she might pull in technical resources as a normal part of the sale, especially if the sale is technical or the application requires engineering or other input. She might accompany this person on the visit and she might not. She's relying on the technical person to not do anything to jeopardize the momentum with the sale. If she can't make the visit she'll need the technical person to relay information to her that might be useful in learning about needs or understanding problems. If the sale advances to a proposal the supplier might have a quote team or proposal preparation team that participates. At another point in the sale the account might want to know that the seller is committing the right resources to the account and wants to hear that from senior executives. Coordinating all of these resources and touch points is complicated any way you look at it.

Getting Sales Data Can Be a Challenge

Another challenge is getting sales data and in a timely manner. You might know what the overall sales number is for the account but not know where the sales are coming from. If the account has multiple locations this gets even more complicated. And without knowing where the business is coming from it's harder to upsell or identify new opportunities.

Multiple Funnel Models

One question I get asked early when we help a client implement a funnel process for national accounts is, do we need one funnel for the national accounts group and another funnel for the salesforce that is calling on the local or regional sites that fall under the contracts? Later in this chapter we'll address this in greater detail. For now, let's set the stage for why it's an issue.

The simplest way to describe the purpose of a national accounts group is that it secures contracts that allow the supplier's salesforce the right to earn new business at the local or regional level. For many national accounts, when a new contract is signed the supplier hasn't really sold anything. The contract is often a 'fishing license' for its salesforce to call on the local facilities or branches or whatever and find new business. Without the contract the supplier may be prohibited from selling, or is strongly discouraged, or at best has an obstacle that makes things more challenging.

Take the hospitals and GPOs for instance. A contract with a GPO gives the manufacturer a right to send its salesforce into the hospitals to look for new sales opportunities. The contract spells out product pricing and terms and conditions. The hospital staff for the most part knows that this contract exists. It still doesn't guarantee sales to the manufacturer for two reasons. One, the hospital might have a similar contract with a second supplier. This gives it a choice and lets the hospital still comply to a GPO contract. Two, the hospital might not have high compliance to its contracts. Its staff buys product off contract. It might even get a better deal when it does so.

The funnel challenges are the manufacturer has one sale to make to secure the contract and a second sale to make to win new business at each of the member hospitals. To be most effective, you want both your national accounts group and field salesforce aligned, on the same selling page. One funnel system promotes that. It's possible that the funnel designs could be different and yet there's no compromise to the alignment.

If you run the salesforce for a retirement services provider and you have a group that secures contracts or agreements with the channel (brokerage firms and advisors) you'd want your field salesforce calling on the advisors at the companies where you have agreements. If not, you're not as likely to penetrate those large brokerage firms and leverage their channel strength.

More Channel Challenges

Another selling challenge that's common to strategic and national accounts has to do with channel issues. Channel issues present many challenges to funnel management because they present many challenges to selling. Having a funnel process doesn't fix all of the challenges and potential conflicts, but it does give manufacturers and their channel partners a way to work through them.

One of my clients sells industrial products through a dealer network, and the dealers sell to end users. The client has done a wonderful job putting process to their funnel management with these dealers. They've shown the dealers how it helps them target the right accounts, penetrate those accounts more effectively, and how it helps both my client and the dealer work better together on the mutual goals of selling more product through the channel. To help them manage the funnel process, they've incorporated our system into a CRM product they use. All of the salespeople can use it to better manage their dealer and other business, and the client's sales management has an overall visibility and reporting capability to value the funnels, forecast, and make better business decisions.

Implementing a Funnel Process – Where to Begin

Because there are some distinct differences in managing and selling to strategic and national accounts you'll want to tailor your funnel process to each type of account. Let's first look at how you could do this with strategic accounts then see how it's done with your national accounts.

Strategic Accounts

One of the places you'll want to start when you implement a funnel process with your strategic accounts is by funneling the account the most efficient way. This is done by knowing how the account is organized.

Learning how the account is organized helps you set up an effective funnel system for a number of reasons. One, since strategic accounts are often large companies and large companies can be more of a challenge to sell to and manage, it helps you break down the larger entity into something more manageable. Second, if you already sell to the account this will help you know where your business is coming from, which lets you better identify the potential in the account overall. Third, your sales strategies will be more effective when you can pinpoint your business and know how the account is organized.

Finally, knowing how the account is organized gives you the right perspective for another reason – it tells you something about how the account buys from you, that is, *what the buying process is for the account*. This mirrors the perspective that we've been touting from the beginning with the BuyCycle Funnel™, the need to know the buying process for the opportunity. It's the right perspective to have for each sales opportunity and it's right for how to strategize for the account.

Let's use a hypothetical scenario to make some points about this.

Example: Kensington Industries

Let's say you're the VP of sales for a company that sells industrial supply products mainly to manufacturing companies of all types. You sell a big catalogue worth of products that are used in the manufacturing process, anything from tools and ladders to buckets and brackets. You have tens of thousands of products. One of your accounts is a company called Kensington Industries, a multi billion dollar global manufacturer of products used in hydraulic, automation, filtration, and otherwise industrial applications. Its customers are found across many industries including automotive, aerospace, food and beverage, packaging, oil and gas, telecommunication, energy, semiconductor, and others. You've been analyzing some of the bigger accounts among your book of business and from a dollar perspective Kensington ranks up there as being one of the largest, about $2M.

You're thinking that Kensington and other large accounts hold great potential for growth. You think that with the proper strategy and tools you could reasonably target 20% growth in these accounts. At Kensington that's another $400,000 of business. If that's reasonable, then there are a few funnel type questions right away you'll want the answers to:

1. If you want another $400,000 of business next year from Kensington how much business will your account managers have to be actively pursuing? Twice that much? Three times? More?

2. Where is this 20% growth going to come from? How much of it can you get from the current divisions and locations you sell to? What about uncovering new selling opportunities at new locations and divisions you don't currently sell to?

3. How do you set up a funnel system to accomplish that growth?

Let's look at Kensington's organization structure.

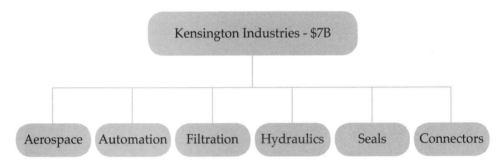

Looking at the organization structure, you pinpoint that your business comes from the hydraulic division only. Plus, it comes from two of three regions within that division. There's a new southeast region that was recently established.

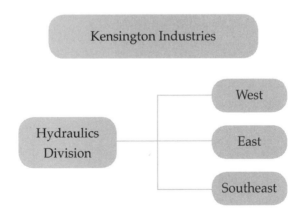

You're planning to meet with each of your account managers that has a Kensington location or facility in their territories and tell them that you intend to put more focus on Kensington and other larger accounts and you need their commitment to working a new system to accomplish that. What you want to do is give your AMs good direction and coaching in how to approach this task – more than simply telling them to 'go spend more time selling to Kensington and work harder in the account'. You begin to set up a funnel process.

The first thing you do is tell all three AMs you'd like to see a report that tells you what opportunities they're currently working on, the dollar value and when they're expected to close. You also ask them to identify additional selling opportunities that they aren't currently working on. For example, your company launched a line of chemical detergents a few months ago and sales of this product line have been very slow.

Two weeks later the AMs come back with the information you requested and you put it into a chart like the one below:

Region	Number of opportunities	Dollar value of all sales opportunities
West	2	75,000
East	1	125,000
Southeast		
Total	3	200,000

When you see this information you're thinking this is a start but it's not enough to get to your target increase of $400,000. Even if you close all 3 deals you'd fall short of hitting the target. You feel that your AMs need to be pursuing 3-4 times the actual dollar value of business you're targeting, based on a gut feel that they close about one out of every three or four sales. With a $400,000 target this means you need them to have at least $1.2M to $1.6M of active sales opportunities among the three AMs. With an average deal size of $60,000 this means you'll need to see between 20 and about 27 active opportunities. You could reduce the number by half if you doubled the average sale value. You have this conversation individually with the three account managers in each region and challenge them to review their books of business to find additional sales opportunities. You tell them you'll be tracking this selling activity weekly for the next several months.

About a month later you get a new report of active sales opportunities from your three AMs which shows new sales opportunities have been uncovered in each of the regions.

Region	Number of opportunities	Dollar value of all sales opportunities
West	5	275,000
East	3	245,000
Southeast	2	90,000
Total	10	610,000

You're pleased, because this is definitely an improvement in the number of opportunities and dollar value being pursued. You'd want to know that the new opportunities are genuinely valid and at what stage of the buying process they're to be found. It's still far short of the dollar value of the opportunities you need them to pursue, but it highlights just how far you have to go.

Your funnel process begins to look something like this:

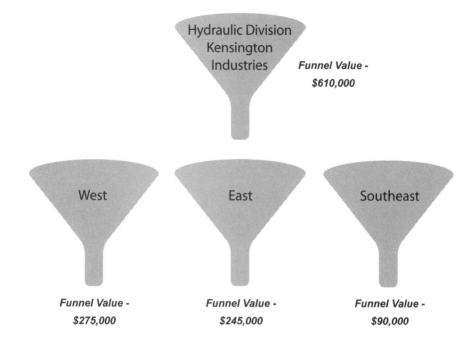

You could also have a Funnel Dashboard for this that looks something like this:

Kensington Industries Funnel Dashboard	
Our Quota for Kensington	$400,000
YTD sales	48,000
GAP	352,000
Total Viable Revenue	225,000
Funnel Shortfall (using 3X benchmark)	831,000
Funnel Factor	0.64

There's a lot more to your funnel process than this, but it's a start. Each AM has a funnel, a dollar value of it, and some targets to shoot for. You've got a handle on the Viable Revenue your AMs are chasing, and unfortunately it's far short of what you need. You've got a long way to go, and you'd likely want to consider adding the following elements to your process:

- Have a standard BuyCycle Funnel™ that all AMs use. This way you can coach effectively to it, you can value the entire strategic accounts funnel, and you can forecast more accurately with it.

- Put these funnels in some kind of excel spreadsheet or use the company's CRM tool to capture the funnels.

- Design some simple funnel reports that show you on demand all the opportunities being pursued, their dollar value, and their place in the customer's buying process.

- Have a Funnel Dashboard for each account manager and each one rolls up to one Funnel Dashboard for all of Kensington.

- Train other staff on the funnel process and give them an incentive to find new opportunities. Service staff for example might uncover new opportunities on routine service calls.

- You could establish a new products funnel as a way to focus attention on selling new products, increase funnel value and impact sales productivity.

- You can target other divisions of the company for new opportunities. Big companies move people around. You might have a contact that once worked in Hydraulics that is now in the Seals or Automation division and can open a door for you to find new business there.

Leveraging the Process

Once you layout the process and get the elements working together, you can consider taking it to the next level if it's appropriate for your company. You bring into the process the other divisions of your own company that might also sell to Kensington. You or someone other than you coordinates the selling efforts of these divisions. Your company takes an even bigger value proposition to Kensington.

Setting Up a Funnel Process for National Accounts

A funnel process for national accounts is similar to one for strategic accounts, but there's one important difference between the two that requires a different funnel approach for national accounts funnels. National accounts has a field salesforce that is deployed as part of the strategy to win business within the contracted accounts at the local territory level. For the most part the role of the national accounts team is to win the right for its field salesforce to go after business at the local level under the contract. Usually it's out of their hands after they've secured the contract. It doesn't mean they're entirely done selling, but the field has to step up and generate business within the local offices and facilities. A funnel system can be an excellent way to manage this business. Let's take a look at businesses in three different industries to see how a funnel process could be set up.

Financial Services

Companies that operate in the financial services industry often require agreements with their providers (suppliers) as a condition for doing business. For example, a company selling its 401K products (the provider) to brokerage firms such as UBS or Raymond James would likely need a selling agreement in place to do so. The provider might have a corporate staff of national accounts managers (sometimes called relationship managers) whose job it is to get agreements signed at the corporate office of the brokerage firm, then the provider's salesforce in the field calls on the advisors in that firm to convince them to use the provider's product with the advisor's clients. These agreements are fishing licenses for the provider – they are not a guarantee of sales. The brokerage firm might have several of these agreements in place with providers.

The provider could have a funnel for its national accounts group and have targets for numbers of agreements to win with the brokerage firms. It could also have a funnel that the field salesforce uses to call on the local branches and the advisors there to get the advisors to recommend the provider's 401K products.

Home Building Industry

Another example of how you can funnel national accounts can be seen in the home building industry. If you're a supplier of products to these companies you'll likely need a contract to sell to the large ones that have offices or branches across the country. Toll Brothers, Centex, and DR Horton sign contracts with home building suppliers that defines supplier pricing and terms and conditions to all of the markets they sell into around the country. The supplier's sales force must then call on the local or regional offices and bid on the business for each of the projects and support that office at the local level.

In this industry it is not uncommon for a builder to have a national contract with one supplier, thereby making it very difficult for non-contracted suppliers to earn business at the local level. The local offices of the national builder might have some leeway to purchase off contract in some cases. Therefore, getting the national contract is more of a guarantee of getting some business.

Setting up a funnel system in this situation can still be valuable. For one, funneling the builders that the national accounts team wants to contract with helps the team work the selling process for each builder. Two, the supplier might have a good idea of the quantity and value of homes the builder will build over a period of time, say 2-3 years. This helps the supplier get closer to valuing the business with that builder and helps the supplier decide which builders to aggressively pursue.

Now let's shift to the field salesforce. If you run national accounts for the supplier you'll want to know that your company's local salespeople are selling to the national builders you've contracted with. You can monitor and even drive this selling activity if you have funnel visibility.

With a funnel visibility for the entire salesforce, you can monitor the mix of business your salesforce is pursuing. For example, if single family home sales starts to slow down and multi family picks up, your funnel can show how much multi family business the salesforce is pursuing. If it's not enough, you'll know that and you can direct the field's selling efforts to pick it up there.

Selling to Hospitals

Selling into hospitals is a third example of where having a funnel system can help the national accounts team and the field salesforce work better together toward the company's common goals.

Hospitals and their affiliated clinics and surgery centers etc. often buy products on contract by using GPOs (Group Purchasing Organizations) or some other kind of buying group to secure product from manufacturers. The hospital pays a GPO to be a member of the GPO and in return the GPO secures special pricing and terms with manufacturers for its member hospitals. If you're a manufacturer and you want to sell to a hospital in St. Louis, and that hospital is a member of some buying group, you'll want to know if it's necessary or really beneficial for you to be on that hospital's contract.

Once you have the contract your company's salesperson in St. Louis is allowed to call on that hospital and try to sell it products.

Similar to the previous two examples, you can have a national accounts contract for all of the GPOs and other buying groups or networks that you want to secure contracts with. And, you'd have a field salesforce funnel of all of the sales opportunities the salespeople are pursuing under each contract.

One Funnel or Two for National Accounts?

A common question for setting up a funnel system for national accounts is should the business use one funnel for getting the contracts and a second one for the business that the field salespeople bring in?

In answering this question it's important to remember that the national accounts team and the field salesforce should be working closely together. Anything you can do to promote alignment between the two to work closer together should be done.

There are two different sales happening. One occurs when national accounts secures the contracts. The second occurs when the field salesforce calls on the local and regional offices, branches or sites and uncovers and wins new business under the contracts. To know if you need two funnel designs, you'll want to analyze the buying process for securing a national contract and do the same for the buying process at the end user. It's possible that the two models can be different and have no adverse effect on your goal of alignment.

Valuing a National Accounts Funnel

When a supplier signs a national contract or agreement it wants to have a good idea of the dollar value of that contract, that is, how much business it can expect to bring in under the contract. If the contract defines how much product the account will purchase and there are penalties to not purchasing that volume, then the contract value is understood. However, if the agreement is just a fishing license, then the supplier can only estimate the contract value. Even an exclusive contract between the account and one supplier, like one you might find in the home building industry, usually doesn't guarantee a volume of sales to the supplier. It's too risky for the builder to lock into those terms.

While it would be nice to have a guaranteed dollar value of the contract upon signing, what you really want to know with your national account business is the same thing you want to know with your other business – the dollar value of the funnel at any time. You want to know if your company's funnel of national accounts business is sufficient to win by the end of the year the amount of national accounts sales you're expecting the contract to produce. And there's no better way to do this than with the funnel. If you're a supplier and you sign a contract worth an estimated $100M and you've sold $30M by June, you've probably got some explaining to do to the corner office. Now, if most of your business comes in the back half of the year, you still might have a chance to hit the target. But wouldn't it be great if you could pull a funnel report in June that showed that the field salesforce had over $200M of Viable Opportunities just for accounts that fall under this national contract? With a 30% hit rate you've got a sporting chance of closing yor $70M GAP. That kind of information would make everyone breathe a little easier.

The only way to know the dollar value of the national accounts funnel is to know the dollar value of all of the sales in progress that fall under all of the contracts among all of your field salespeople. This has to be done by tracking this business in your sales and funnel reporting, again, just like you would do it when funneling the rest of your business.

Let's look at an example of how this might work.

Example: Millennium Buying Group

Let's say you're the national accounts director of a manufacturer of medical products sold to hospitals. You have three national account managers reporting to you. The salesforce has one hundred people in it, reporting up to ten District Managers who report to four Regional Vice Presidents. Your group signed a three year contract worth an estimated $100M per year with a buying group called Millennium. It gives you the right to sell to the fifty hospitals that are members of the Millennium buying group. This business is not a guaranteed $100M per year but based on historical and projected usage of your types of products at these hospitals – it's been about $175M a year - you feel that $100M per year is a very reasonable target. Even though it's a dual source contract – one other supplier is also contracted with this account - you feel good about hitting this target because you know what your field salesforce is capable of selling.

Since you're a funnel expert, you've set up some process for managing this business. You want to know, and be able to show your boss, the President of the division, throughout the year how the company is doing toward that annual revenue target and how likely it is to hit the target. Right now, you're looking at the first quarter sales data.

You've asked the IT department to tag all sales in each territory that fall under this contract. It's not that hard they say. You know the fifty hospitals that are under Millennium's buying group. Any sales to those fifty hospitals gets tagged as a sale under the contract. IT can sort using this criteria and run reports for you. The tricky part is getting a funnel of active sales opportunities among all of the one hundred salespeople. They don't report directly to you – they report to the VP of Sales. And she's yet to install a funnel process. However, you have a good working relationship with her and she gives you her support in getting each Region Vice President to give you the number of sales opportunities by territory and the dollar value of those opportunities. Two weeks later you have that information. You take it and create a funnel dashboard using the sales figures IT gave you and it looks like this:

West Region	
Quota	25,000,000
Year to date	3,000,000
GAP	22,000,000
TVR	15,000,000
Funnel Shortfall	51,000,000
FF	0.68

East Region	
Quota	25,000,000
Year to date	9,000,000
GAP	16,000,000
TVR	32,000,000
Funnel Shortfall	16,000,000
FF	2.0

Midwest Region	
Quota	25,000,000
Year to date	8,000,000
GAP	17,000,000
TVR	45,000,000
Funnel Shortfall	6,000,000
FF	2.6

South Region	
Quota	25,000,000
Year to date	7,000,000
GAP	18,000,000
TVR	24,000,000
Funnel Shortfall	30,000,000
FF	1.3

You roll up the four regions and create a funnel dashboard for the entire national account, which looks like this:

Millennium	
Quota	100,000,000
Year to date	27,000,000
GAP	73,000,000
TVR	116,000,000
Funnel Shortfall	103,000,000
FF	1.59

This tells you a number of things. One, year to date sales through the first quarter is $27M. TVR (Total Viable Revenue) is $116M of Viable Opportunities at Millennium hospitals across the country. That might sound like a lot, but when you compare it the quota GAP you see that it's slightly more than one and a half times the GAP. In other words, for every dollar left to close to hit that $100M annual target, the salesforce is pursuing about a dollar and a half worth of Viable Opportunities. That might be ok if the hit rate for a Viable Opportunity was 66% - one out of every one and a half. But for your salesforce it's really 33% - they win one out of every three they pursue. The only way the salesforce will achieve the $100M target with this funnel is by increasing its hit rate to 66%. (That's a 100% increase in hit rate, by the way). If it can increase the size of the Viable Opportunities over the coming months it stands a better chance of achieving the quota.

The Funnel Gives You Leading Indicator Information

This example shows you how the funnel can give you *leading indicator* information versus lagging indicator information.

Tracking year to date sales at Millennium hospitals throughout the year can be helpful. But because sales is a lagging indicator, it's of limited value for future planning and funnel managing. Sales data is information about something you can't do anything about, the past. Further, sales data for accounts that fall under a national accounts category might not be available for 45 or 60 days after the sales are made. Funnel data, on the other hand, specifically Total Viable Revenue, is real time information about sales in progress. You know that a certain percentage of TVR will become sales, determined by your hit rate. If the TVR number times your hit rate is not sufficient to close the remaining quota GAP, then you do something about that – provided you're looking at the data early enough in the year.

Let's say you learn in August that 6 months of sales data through June is lagging your expected budget by 23%. Learning this in August means you have barely four months to change course. Rather than waiting until August for June sales numbers to come out, you can look to your funnel's TVR number in June to know if your salesforce is pursuing enough opportunities – and give your salesforce two extra months to change course if it has to.

Summary

With strategic account or national account business being so important to many suppliers, it's good business to invest in sales process for these types of customers. Putting a funnel process focus on earning even more business from these accounts can go a long way toward protecting and growing profitable revenue in your most important customers.

Part Five:

Achieving World Class Competency in BuyCycle Funnel™ Management

Chapter 10

Achieving a World Class Funnel Competency

By now, you know that there's a lot more to funnel management than simply having a sales funnel. To experience breakthrough results in sales, you need the right perspective on the funnel. First, a perspective that recognizes that the funnel holds a ton of potential for accomplishing your sales objectives. That the funnel is the core of the process, but not the process itself. That funnel management isn't your software, or your account list or anything else that is less than a total, comprehensive solution to the business function of finding, qualifying and winning net new business day after day.

That there aren't 50 other books or even five dedicated to funnel management, and that there aren't consulting or training companies with a pure funnel management niche and expertise serving the market tells me this kind of strategic perspective on the funnel isn't widely held. Personally I'm not fine with that. We've got to do a better job of educating sales people and leaders on the importance and potential of the funnel. Maybe you're now one more person who sees this potential. If you are, I'm confident your business and sales results will improve and you'll have one more competitive edge over those that don't adopt the perspective.

What I've been proposing throughout the book is based on what I've seen happen with my clients who are committing to a BuyCycle

Funnel™ process. These are well-known, well-managed companies that are respected and envied by their competitors. They've learned over time as I have that the funnel holds a lot of potential, the BuyCycle Funnel™ is a better funnel model to build process around, and committing to a funnel management process is worth the effort.

I've also painted a picture of the effort needed to commit to a funnel process. In an earlier chapter I outlined several fundamentals of building that process that you'll need to seriously consider. Because connecting those fundamentals and making them work is difficult, companies that begin the journey can easily fall short of the commitment required and never realize the full potential of the funnel. But as I said at the beginning of Part Three, it's not just about the funnel. Now you know what I mean.

The Breakthrough Belief - Putting It All Together

One way to summarize my view of the funnel role and potential and to give you the clearest possible path to breaking through to world class funnel competency is with the Breakthrough Belief™. Breakthrough Belief™ simply unites process, design and integration to unlock the funnel's potential to achieve sales success. It encompasses three vital parts:

1. A comprehensive 8-Step Funnel Management Process that provides strategic dimension to your sales funnel competency.

2. The innovative BuyCycle™ Funnel design that is based on the customer's buying cycle rather than your selling activities.

3. The integration of the 8-Step Funnel Management Process with the BuyCycle Funnel™ design to most effectively and consistently achieve sales success.

As the Breakthrough Belief™ ensures that you are taking the right approach to funnel competency, our 8-Step Funnel Management

Process takes you from strategy to funnel design, to training, coaching and development, to a complete assessment before, during and after the process. Breakthrough is involved with you at every step of the process.

Let's look at the 8-Step model.

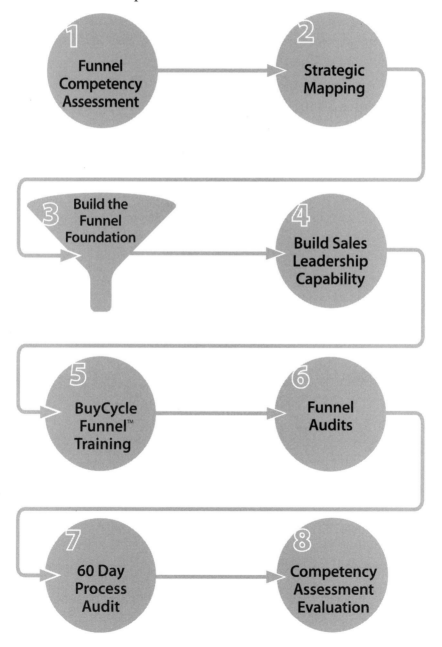

Step 1 - Funnel Competency Assessment

For funnel management to really make a difference in your sales performance you can't just try to get better. You need to set some targets for what getting better looks like and you need to know – and celebrate – when getting better has been achieved. Of course, to get better you'll need to know how good you are right now, where you're starting from. When you know where you're starting and where you're aiming to go you can be smarter about what you need to do to get there. Breakthrough assesses your company's funnel competency across several key measures and identifies your strengths and weaknesses. This gives you a baseline for your current situation and a starting point for defining what to do to improve the competency.

Step 2 - Strategic Mapping

To align your funnel activities with your corporate sales objectives, you'll want to create a strategic map that links these sales objectives to the funnel management process. This step clearly defines the role that a funnel management process plays for the business overall. For example, if you're launching a new product you likely have a target revenue and budget to achieve. You might also have questions about your salesforce's commitment to giving this product the selling time it needs to achieve the objectives. You'll want to use funnel strategy to make sure you manage this activity.

Step 3 - Build the Funnel Foundation

Having a BuyCycle Funnel™ is one of the three parts of the Breakthrough Belief. It's necessary - not optional - to make the funnel system pay off. We take our BuyCycle Funnel™ template and create a custom BuyCycle Funnel™ for your company that serves as the core component of your funnel process. The BuyCycle Funnel™ is designed around the customer's buying or decision-making process, not around your selling activities. It incorporates your selling activities by matching them to the appropriate funnel stage. The result is a design that keeps you focused on how the customer is making the decision for each sale. This design also makes possible an accurate valuation of the funnel by preventing opportunities to be labeled as further along the process than they really are.

Step 4 - Build Sales Leadership Capability

We've learned that the sales managers who work with the salespeople day in and day out play the most pivotal role in the 8-Step model. Their influence can determine whether or not the entire process pays off. It's a big burden to carry, but there's really no shortcut to this step. These managers have moments every day, every week throughout the year to add to or subtract from their people increasing their funnel competency. In many cases managers will have to break old and strong habits to get some salespeople to change their ways. For others who might be more willing but needing a different focus of coaching, the managers have to constantly reinforce the BuyCycle behaviors to help these salespeople adopt and get to the next level. Through a series of training events and coaching, sales managers learn fundamentals of coaching to the BuyCycle Funnel™. They learn the role and responsibility of the coach. They learn how to manage and analyze funnels and how to help salespeople create 30/60/90 day funnel action plans.

Step 5 - BuyCycle Funnel™ Training

The organization will need to get trained in the fundamentals of the BuyCycle Funnel™ and learn how to make your company's custom BuyCycle Funnel™ the core of its selling. In the training, your sales teams participate in a funnel populating workshop and learn to conduct their first Funnel Audit. If your company uses a CRM software or something simple like excel spreadsheets to enter funnel data, you'll want to get your new BuyCycle Funnel™ stages entered in the tool quickly so salespeople can use the tool and the BuyCycle Funnel™ to manage and sell.

Step 6 - Funnel Audits

A Funnel Audit is an inspection of your funnel that is intended to answer one important question: what is my funnel's ability right now to close enough business to achieve my quota? It gives a salesperson and manager an important snapshot of the funnel's condition that helps the salesperson stay on top of changes in sales opportunities that could affect hitting the year-end quota. The Funnel Audit is used to create and execute 30/60/90 day action plans. We recommend that the manager conduct these Audits with his or her salespeople on a scheduled basis to stay on top of changes that are likely to occur to the salesperson's funnel. By knowing about these changes early the salesperson is in a position to act on them to stay on track to hitting sales objectives.

Step 7 - 60 day Process Audit

Because it's so important to quickly begin implementing BuyCycle Funnel™ management after training and coaching and designing the custom BuyCycle Funnel™, it's helpful to measure your progress early to make sure you're on track. Up to now we've completed all of the necessary steps to building the infrastructure to getting to a world class funnel competency. The payoff begins to occur once you get into the rhythm of doing Funnel Audits and selling the BuyCycle way and promoting BuyCycle dialogue and relying on the good funnel data your process is now providing.

Step 8 - Competency Assessment Evaluation

Developing a world class funnel competency requires ongoing assessment of your company's funnel effectiveness. Mid-year and year-end funnel competency assessments are compared to previous assessments to determine progress made and actionable next steps.

This 8-Step Funnel Management Process simplifies the approach you need to take to achieve world class funnel competency.

The Science of Sales, Or Just a Better Approach

One of the movements happening in sales is to make it more of a science. Breakthrough is in the middle of that as we break down the business function of funnel management into its working parts, and then give you a system for being more productive and more efficient at the parts and the whole overall.

The Process might be part science, but I prefer to think of the BuyCycle Funnel™ and the 8-Step Process more as a simple, powerful tool and way of managing that lets you be more productive, more reliable and more successful in sales. The success I've seen clients have with the BuyCycle has been validating and humbling. I'm sure it will help you be more successful too.

The science of selling has to sound odd to some people. Years ago, my father in law sold brick across the United States by driving his car hundreds of miles each week, meeting people, listening to their needs, recommending solutions, and taking orders. He called those orders in by phone, not by PC. He had no internet to do company research and he didn't carry a Blackberry. The fax machine as we know it today hadn't been invented. He looked those customers in the eyes and promised to deliver - and they knew they could count on him to deliver what he promised.

While much of selling will always be something that occurs between two people, the salesperson and the customer, there's no denying that the enterprise continues to influence what the individual salesperson does. The pace of technology, the speed of change, the global markets, the instant-ness of communication, the teaming of salespeople and their support, all make selling different today from those days when my father-in-law plied his trade. Salespeople aren't the lone rangers they once could be. Today they have to work together with other departments. They have to feed information to management timely and accurately so management can make good business decisions. They have to know enough about product and application, and know enough to bring in expert product and application resources to help close business. They're more specialized in a way. This profession of selling is looking more like a profession all the time.

The job of selling doesn't rest with just the salesperson. Therefore, businesses need a way to bring together all the parties involved in selling so the enterprise can sell better, sell more, and be more successful. The funnel is the one element common to these parties, and the BuyCycle Funnel™ and the 8-Step Process is the link that unites them and makes them more productive and more successful.

Incremental Improvement But Dramatic Impact

You won't be surprised when I say that once my clients understand the role that the funnel can play in their business many of them express an interest in getting started right away in getting better at funnel management. But before they rush into a flurry of activity and training and such, I've got to get my sales leaders to slow down and approach this funnel management improvement goal the right way. They need to eventually understand the fundamentals I presented in the earlier chapter, but all of this effort and investment in funnel management is aimed at achieving a world class funnel competency. It's not only the goal but also the constant state you'll want your sales organization to be in. There, the organization is performing at a high level on the sales behaviors that our system has identified as critical to excel in. It's about connecting your overall sales objectives to your funnel management activities. It's about leveraging the funnel to get national accounts and your field based salespeople working more efficiently to target and close new business. It's about increasing sales within your strategic accounts, predictably and methodically. It's about saying goodbye to wildly missed forecasts. It's about elevating everyone's funnel competency through strategy and execution. Bringing everyone up to a higher standard gives you better access to better funnel data which you can use to give your company a competitive edge.

Businesses are always looking for ways to be better, faster, more efficient, and more competent than their competitors. The edge doesn't have to be that great to have a great dramatic difference in outcome. Take any horse race where the margin of victory is sometimes a nose – compared to the mile and a half length of the race a horse's nose isn't that long! But the payout to the winning horse over 2nd place can be substantial. In the Tour de France many stages are won by the length of half a wheel, with the winning cyclist stretching his bike across the finish line at the last moment. After riding for several hours over brutally punishing mountain terrain, often for over 130 miles, it must be exhilarating to finish first – and heart breaking to lose by that margin of half a wheel. Winners are remembered for winning a Tour stage the rest of their careers while no one remembers who came in second.

In fact, in sales, they call second place the first place loser. A tough label I agree, but an accurate one. To the victor goes the spoils. Second place gets no commission.

Having a world class competency in funnel management is every bit worth the effort and investment similar to the investments other parts of the business make to get their own competitive edge. Lean manufacturing, Six Sigma, TQM, are common in well managed companies and normally directed at manufacturing, operations, or supply chain – but seldom sales.

In a 1999 paper published by the Harvard Business Review, Danny Ertel wrote of the need for companies to have a corporate capability for negotiating. He pointed out that a company's employees are engaging in negotiations all the time. Their effectiveness should not be limited to the individual's skills and competency in negotiating, but rather, could be strengthened through a corporate wide negotiation approach that all employees become good at. With negotiations taking place every day throughout the year, ineffectively negotiating can have a significant impact on the company's overall results, one person and one negotiation at a time. For large companies the number can be huge. But you don't have to be a huge company to feel the impact.

It's the same for sales funnel management. Each salesperson's funnel is one part of the overall company funnel. You either add to its integrity or you subtract from it. While one salesperson's inaccurate funnel might have a small effect on the overall business, a hundred inaccurate funnels can really ruin a VP of Sales's day. All of these territory funnels roll up to one business funnel for the VP, and when some or much of that funnel data is bad it makes it hard to make good business decisions on it. They're handicapped from the start. If you've got one salesperson with a funnel value overstated by $100,000 you might be able to live with that. But what if you have 20 or 50 or 100 or 500 salespeople with overstated funnels? Your $100,000 problem could be a ten million or fifty million dollar problem. You know this is not a good way to run a business.

So this is why I'm passionate about our funnel process and it's what I'm trying to get you and your organization to begin adopting.

As I stated in the opening chapter, the most common and most pressing need expressed to me by sales people, their managers and their senior sales leaders is the need to find, qualify, and win new business day after day. A lack of performance with this is what keeps them up at night. And yet, the solution is straightforward, simple, and even intuitive. The payoff is big and you can have fun at the same time. After all, hitting your numbers is always a blast, isn't it?

Common Questions

Over the years I've had many questions asked about the BuyCycle Funnel™ and the 8-Step Process for making it work. Here are the most common questions and their answers.

Why is the BuyCycle Funnel™ called the New Standard™?

It's called the New Standard™ for two reasons. One, it addresses the shortcomings or flaws of the type of funnel that is most commonly used in business today, what I call the Traditional funnel. Two, because it's a better design it should replace the Traditional funnel as the design of choice and become the new standard in the trade.

What's wrong with the old standard or traditional approach to funnel management?

The main flaw of the Traditional funnel is the funnel stages are defined by selling activity. This promotes a focus on selling activity instead of the customer's buying process or buying cycle which can lead the salesperson to unproductive selling behavior. It also promotes an overvaluation of the funnel which causes many problems.

Isn't the funnel just something that most good software products offer?

Software is not a funnel. The software is the tool to run reports and provide visibility to a funnel.

Why is commitment so important to the BuyCycle Funnel™ model?

Commitment is necessary for a person or a company to make a purchase decision. You can get a prospect to agree there are problems, or agree that he or she would like to make a change, but until that prospect commits to activities to change it'll be status quo and you won't sell a thing.

What industries has the BuyCycle Funnel™ been validated in?

Consumer goods, industrial products, large equipment sales, professional services, many areas of healthcare including hospital sales, long term care markets, GPO environments, software products and services, financial services, automotive.

Are there any industries or types of businesses where the BuyCycle Funnel™ will not work well?

The BuyCycle Funnel™ is applicable for any industry and type of business that operates in a business to business environment.

Are there any channel models where it won't work well?

The BuyCycle Funnel™ has been effective in different channel models such as direct sales to the end user, through distribution, dealers, and advisor channels in financial services. It's been used to provide value added services by manufacturers to its channel partners.

Regarding the stage definitions, when a customer is in a BuyCycle Funnel™ stage of its buying process, does that mean the customer has completed that stage? Can a customer be in a stage a little bit or in the stage a lot?

If a customer has reached a stage, it is fully engaged in that stage of its decision making process or buying cycle. However, this means that the customer might still be working through issues and development in that stage before advancing to the next stage. For example, when a customer has reached Define Economic Consequence it means the customer has not only Recognized a Problem, it is actively engaged in defining the economics of this problem. Consider this: the customer can advance to Commit Funding and still not know everything it wants to know about the economics of the problem, but it knows enough about the economics of the problem to Commit Funding. Later, throughout the rest of the buying process the customer might learn even more about the economics of the problem.

Can the BuyCycle Funnel™ work in a transactional type selling environment with one buying influence over one or two sales calls?

Maybe, but our experience is not in this environment so we can't say yes for sure.

Can the BuyCycle Funnel™ work with other selling methods?

Absolutely. It is method 'neutral' and has been integrated with several different methods such as Strategic Selling and Conceptual Selling from Miller Heiman, Solution Selling, SPIN Selling, and Counselor Selling.

There's a rule of thumb or 'generally accepted principle' that says when you close a piece of business you should replace that with a certain number of new prospects. How does the BuyCycle treat this?

First of all, this is a wonderful rule of thumb. You'll seldom go wrong adopting this mentality. That said, the BuyCycle takes a slightly more reasoned approach to the answer. It all goes back to quota achievement and Total Viable Revenue. For example, if you've reached your quota should you replace that closed business with new prospects? Why should you? If you have accelerators to higher commissions beyond 100% of quota then it might make sense to do that to make more money. But the fact is you've reached your sales quota for the fiscal period and technically you don't need to close anything else. Also, if you already have a ton of Viable opportunities, more than your target Total Viable Revenue, then why invest time in prospecting when you've got sufficient Viable Revenue that could become closed business? The BuyCycle Funnel™

helps you be smarter about how much prospecting and new lead generation you need to do.

Is it possible to still achieve your quota when your funnel is not at Target TFR?

Yes. But only if something significant changes about your funnel management – your close rate. If you haven't achieved quota, you have a GAP. The only way to close the GAP fully (achieve quota) is to have enough Total Viable Revenue to let your historical close rate kick in and close the necessary percentage of business to close the GAP. Or, if your close rate somehow increases and you close a higher percentage of TVR (a TVR number that would be insufficient with your historical close rate).

The BuyCycle Sales Funnel avoids overstating funnel value by not 'dollarizing' opportunities that haven't reached the Viable stage of Commit Funding. Can't we accomplish the same thing with a traditional funnel by applying a zero dollar value to the NonViables?

No. A traditional funnel doesn't prevent you from placing opportunities further down the funnel than they belong because the funnel's stages are still defined by selling activity. For example, you might say let's count the dollar value of the sale toward our funnel value when you've delivered a proposal. But just because you deliver a proposal, even at a customer's request, doesn't mean that the dollar value should be counted. It's possible that the person with financial authority for this purchase has not committed to spending money yet.

Is the BuyCycle Funnel™ a forecasting tool or system?

Though it's not a forecasting system it makes possible accurate forecasting. The BuyCycle Funnel™ gives you better funnel data. You identify in your forecasting system the stage or stages that you'll include in the forecast.

The BuyCycle Funnel™ says you cannot include in the dollar value of the funnel revenue any opportunities that have yet to reach Commit Funding. Why not just apply a low percentage to the dollar value of deals that are at NonViable stages?

The problem with including in your Total Viable Revenue any dollar value of the opportunities that are NonViable is first, these opportunities are not sufficiently developed to be considered Viable. They still have too low a likelihood of becoming an order not just for you but for any company. Second, often these NonViable opportunities are so early in development the salesperson is unable to accurately put a dollar value on them. Finally, including the dollar value for NonViables doesn't help you in an appreciable way to manage your funnel.

References

Harvard Business Review is a bi-monthly, scholarly business publication based in Boston, MA. I reference it in several places throughout the book, including the Thomas Bonoma paper in 1982 and a salesforce productivity paper in Sept. 2006.

The New Solution Selling is a book authored by Keith M. Eades and is published by McGraw-Hill, copyright 2004.

Good to Great is authored by Jim Collins and is published by Harper Collins, copyright 2001.

Organizational Buying Behavior was authored by Frederick E. Webster, Jr., and Yoram Wind. It appeared in the Journal of Marketing, Vol. 37, No. 4 (October 1973), p. 122.

Jagdish N. Sheth, Ph.D is a professor of Marketing at Goizueta Business School of Emory University in Atlanta, GA. He is credited with researching the field of buyer behavior as a graduate student at the University of Pittsburgh. While there, he studied under John Howard and together they published work under the field of Theory of Buyer Behavior.

Roger Blackwell is often called the father of consumer behavior. In 1968 he and two other professors at Ohio State University created a model of consumer behavior called the EKB Model named after its three authors (David Kollat, Roger Blackwell, Jim Engle).

Jim Dickie is CEO of Insight Technology Group. Its major study of over 1400 CRM implementations is referenced in chapter 5.

Miller Heiman Inc. is a sales training company based in Reno, NV. Its well known sales training courses include Strategic Selling, Conceptual Selling, and LAMP. The Strategic Selling book is copyrighted 1985 by Warner Business Books. It's Sales Effectiveness Study is mentioned in chapter 5.

SPIN Selling is a book and course authored by Neil Rackham and published by MCGraw-Hill, copyright 1988.

SAMA is the Strategic Account Management Association. Based in Chicago, SAMA is dedicated to furthering the mission of helping companies and executives understand and apply best practices to their management of strategic accounts.

Wilson Learning is a sales training company based in Minnesota.

Dale Carnegie is a sales training and personal development company.

Brian Tracy is a best-selling author, speaker and consultant for personal and business success.

Key Account Management and Planning is authored by Noel Capon and is published by Free Press, copyright 2001

Mr. Bridgewater in chapter 7 is a fake name for a real client of mine.

Index

About the Author and Breakthrough

Mark Sellers is founder and CEO of Breakthrough Sales Performance LLC, an innovative sales consulting firm. Consulting with corporate leaders worldwide, Mark is recognized for his ability to help companies make wholesale changes to their selling processes and understands that the key to successful selling is through the management of the sales process as a whole, with training and funnel competency playing vital roles in sales success.

Mark founded Breakthrough in 1996. His active clients include Whirlpool Corp., Smith & Nephew, Goodyear, Mass Mutual, Honeywell, T. Rowe Price, Cardinal Health, Tenneco, and Cott Systems. Mark empowers his clients to become self-sufficient with their sales processes. While the Breakthrough Belief™ and the BuyCycle Funnel™ Management™ process are structured sales programs, Mark customizes these programs for each client engagement.

Mark is available for consulting and speaking opportunities. You can email Mark at mark@breakthrough-sales.com or phone him at 614.571.8267. Please visit Breakthrough's website for more information and products on funnel management at www.breakthrough-sales.com.